Who Cares
What You're Supposed To Do?

Breaking the Rules to Get
What You Want in Love, Life, and Work

VICTORIA C. DICKERSON, PH.D.
WITH CARLA FINE

A PERIGEE BOOK

A Perigee Book
Published by The Berkley Publishing Group
A division of Penguin Group (USA) Inc.
375 Hudson Street
New York, New York 10014

Perigee trade paperback edition: August 2004

Visit our website at www.penguin.com

Library of Congress Cataloging-in-Publication Data

Dickerson, Victoria C.
    Breaking the rules : deciding who you are, in your own time and on your own
terms /Victoria C. Dickerson and Carla Fine.
        p. cm.
    ISBN 0-399-52999-3
    1. Women—Psychology. 2. Young women—Psychology. 3. Self-doubt.
4. Expectation (Psychology) 5. Social pressure. I. Fine, Carla. II. Title.

HQ1206.D513 2004
158'.084'22–dc22   2003069644

PRINTED IN THE UNITED STATES OF AMERICA

10   9   8   7   6   5   4   3   2   1

Who Cares
What You're Supposed To Do?

Breaking the Rules to Get
What You Want in Love, Life, and Work

to my goddaughter
Brandy C. Lee-Jacob

CONTENTS

ACKNOWLEDGMENTS

I WOULD LIKE to think the ideas in this book are original, but I know that, rather, they are the culmination of all that I have learned from the many allies I have the privilege to know. These allies include not only my family, friends, and colleagues, but also the many women and men who have shared their lives with me. My intention is to be inclusive in my acknowledgments, but invariably and inadvertently someone who has touched my life may go unnamed. Nonetheless, I am grateful to you all.

It is my family and friends who sustain me. My late mother Violet was and is my strongest ally, who during the years when she was widowed and alone stood steadfast with me as I was struggling to find my way. My dear friend, Kaethe Weingarten, encouraged me from the beginning, helped create a template for how to think about my ideas, suggested that I include a section about "allies," and continues to check on how I am doing. Her heartfelt friendship and shared knowledge give me ongoing hope and faith. Helen Gremillion thought through concepts with me and made crucial suggestions. She is a presence in my life. My sisters: Diane Bird patiently read early drafts, virtually held my hand when I was upset, and allows me to have whatever emotions I have; and Teresa McGinnis continually pushes me to clarify my thoughts and believe in myself. My late father, "Dick," always told me I could do anything I wanted to do—and I believed him.

The women and men directly associated with this book include Jim Levine, who was willing to take a chance on an unknown writer with a good idea. My agent Stephanie Kip-Rostan shepherded the process from original idea to final draft, staying with me all the way and resulting in a finished product that was more than I ever dreamed. My writer Carla Fine consistently prodded me to clarify my thinking and expression; her thoughtful rewriting turned a mass of ideas and stories into a carefully crafted reader-friendly book. Sheila Curry Oakes, my editor, was able to cut to the heart of the message and bring it to the fore.

I want to acknowledge the wonderful women who enrich my life: Rachel Hare-Mustin, whose insightful humor delights me; Evan Imber-Black, my longtime mentor and friend; Dorothea Lewis, Aileen Cheshire, and Meg Northcote, my New Zealand critics and hiking buddies; Jill Freedman, Melissa Elliott, Maria Flores, Janet Adams-Westcott, Lisa Berndt, Ann Epston, Johnella Bird, Cheryl White, Kiwi Tamasese, Deirdre Evans-Pritchard, and Kitty Moore, all of whom I can call on at any time. My nieces, Miki Bird, Dani Bird Voeller, and Joanne Muessle Chidester delight me at every turn. My longtime ally, Patricia Sequeira Belvel; and my local network, Jan Brennan, Katie Beckett, Judy McCormack, Cindy Jouras, Davece Pires, LeAnn Berg, and my many golf partners who stuck with me through the writing process.

I especially honor all the women who have consulted me and who have taught me what it is like to be a woman in her twenties and early thirties in this twenty-first century, the women whose stories I've drawn on for this book: Shelby, Amberlin, Gina, Sara, Shannon, Jenna, Molly, Lisa, Gloria, Joan, Ursula, Kerry, Kelly, Anna, Sylvia, and countless others who are creating lives of their own choosing.

I am grateful to the men in my life: those with whom I've shared ideas, teaching and learning experiences, golf, baseball, long walks, and much laughter. David Epston, who always encourages me; John Neal, a co-teacher and constant supporter; Jeff Zimmerman, former partner in teaching, writing, business, and baseball fanaticism; Bill Lax and Stephen Madigan, my Narrative on Tour and planet-therapy cohorts; Michael White, from whom I first learned narrative ideas; Bill Madsen, Colin Sanders, Gene Combs, Charles Waldegrave, Ian Law, Nigel Pizzini, Ken Hardy, David Nyland, Jay Lappin, and Ronnie Swartz are all among the men I love. My nephews, Marty Bird and Eric Bird; my brothers-in-law, Mike Bird and Bob McGinnis, are men who are by my side. My support group on the homefront includes David Pires, Mitch Ronning, Grady Jeter, Brant Wilson, and Eddie Spencer, backing me completely.

I want to make special mention of the woman to whom this book is dedicated, Brandy Lee-Jacob. She shared with me her self-doubts and her successes as she navigated the terrain of her twenties. She is my best teacher in this regard. I thank you for what you have taught me.

The Pressure to Do Everything

TAKE A MINUTE to think about how you're feeling right now. Does it sometimes seem as if you're just "doing" your life? Are you worried that things might not be working out the way you want? Do you even know what you want or where you should be at this point in your life?

If this sounds familiar, don't worry—you are not alone. When women in their twenties leave home or college and start doing what they assume is expected of them, they often get twinges of fear or discontent or sadness. They—and you—probably try not to pay too much attention to those twinges: It feels too threatening and you'd rather not think about it.

Putting your head in the sand or pulling the covers over your head will only work for so long: The twinges continue to pop up just when you least expect them. In the middle of taking a shower, running off to the gym, or going to work, you may start to feel anxious. You have trouble breathing, your heart is pounding, but you tell yourself, "I can't think about this now."

Or, it's Friday afternoon and you realize you haven't made any plans for the weekend. You call several of your friends, but everyone is already booked. You start wondering, "Why didn't they include me? Am I that boring to be around?"

Or, you meet a nice guy and spend a few weeks hanging out together. You're having fun, so you assume he is too. Then all of a sudden he stops calling you or quits answering your e-mails. "What did I do wrong?" you ask yourself. "I was sure he liked me."

As a clinical psychologist, I constantly hear these worries and concerns from the young women I work with: They are feeling tremendous pressure from the expectation they experience as the need to "do everything." They are constantly being reminded that the world is filled with great promise and possibility where they can seemingly pick and choose what they want to do with their lives. However, the reality is, what seem like options and opportunities feel like pressures and expectations.

The insecurity, anxiety, and dissatisfaction that women like you in their twenties and early thirties are experiencing is what I call self-doubt. It makes you unable to see clearly or think straight, let alone make decisions or changes in your life. Self-doubt is the effect of the tremendous pressure you feel to meet a certain set of expectations that come from society and are passed on and reaffirmed by your parents, your friends, and most of all, yourself. These require you to accomplish a series of goals in both your personal and professional lives that are to be attained within an expected time frame—career by twenty-five, marriage by thirty, baby by thirty-five, and so on.

Where do these expectations come from? Who made them up? Young women of today are living with the legacy of feminism, and the change in a woman's role in the world is permanently interwoven in the fabric of every aspect and institution of our society. The message you hear from the media, your parents, teachers, bosses, friends, and coworkers—not to mention the guy you may be dating—is consistent: Get married and have children, but also accomplish a great many other goals as well.

As you know, marriage is just the beginning of what is expected of you. Somewhere along the line, the once-empowering message "Women can do anything" has morphed into the mandate "Women must do everything."

So where does this leave you? Like every other generation of women before you, you're supposed to get married and have children. But it doesn't stop there. The twentysomething woman must also pursue a career and all those other things in life that lead to "independence." Now, you are expected to:

1. **Get a Man:** Get married and have children—or at least become involved in a meaningful relationship that will eventually lead to a commitment.

2. **Have a Career:** Find a job you have "passion" for and that will eventually lead to a career.

3. **Make It on Your Own:** Become financially independent and self-sufficient.

4. Look Good, Be Thin: Stay attractive, pay special attention to your appearance, and keep fit.

5. Be Popular: Create an active social life and have tons of friends.

6. Leave the Nest: Strike out on your own and have your own life.

7. Follow the Rules: Do it *right* and in a timely fashion, even if you're not sure it's exactly what you really want.

The pressure to fulfill all these expectations can be incredibly stressful and overwhelming. If you can't or don't want to accomplish every item on this list, you assume that something must be wrong with you. You begin to doubt yourself and your abilities—not only in the specific area where you think you have "failed," but also about your life in general. And the more you question what you want and can do, the more confused you become.

"Regardless of their levels of self-esteem, confidence, and overall well-being, twentysomethings are particularly vulnerable to doubts," write Alexandra Robbins and Abby Wilner in their best-selling book, *Quarterlife Crisis*. "They doubt their decisions, their abilities, their readiness, their past, present, and future. . . . Many times the doubts increase because twentysomethings think it is abnormal to have them in the first place. No one talks about having doubts at this age, so when twentysomethings do find that they are continuously questioning themselves, they think something is wrong with them."

That's the bad news. The good news is that there are ways to deal with these doubts and paths you can follow to free yourself from the pressure created by these expectations. By making decisions with self-confidence rather than self-doubt and addressing the fear as well as your real experience, you will be able to create the changes you desire and live the life you want.

In the following pages, I will show you how to understand the difference between self-doubt, which prevents you from paying attention to what you really want, and your own intuition, which lets you question and make decisions by listening to a conviction deep within yourself. I will also help you learn skills and techniques to recognize and overcome self-doubt, and begin to reclaim power over your life. Remember: (1) Self-doubt does not come from you. (2) You can conquer self-doubt and not give into it. (3) You can transform self-doubt by challenging the expectations in your life, believing in yourself, and deciding what you want.

As you start to distinguish between what you want for yourself and the expectations others have of you, you will see that many of these expectations are actually things you do want for yourself—but on your own terms. By learning to trust your own intuition, you will begin to feel comfortable—and confident—with the choices you make and the changes you decide on.

Throughout this book, I will help you to do the following:

- **Recognize and name the problem.** You'll learn how to recognize what is bothering you and put a name to it—self-doubt, insecurity, feeling wrong, fear, lack of trust, or whatever feels like the "right" name for you. Once you give the problem a name and identity, you will see that its power over you can begin to diminish.

• **Understand and challenge the expectation.** You'll come to understand that the problem is self-doubt and not you; the problem is the effect of the pressure you're experiencing from the expectations you face. Learning new techniques as well as remembering your own skills will help you challenge these expectations from a position of confidence and clarity.

• **Connect to what you value and believe.** By acknowledging your skills and gifts as well as recalling past episodes of success and confidence, you will begin to connect to what you know about yourself and to what you value and believe. As you bring your unique talents into the present, you will be able to live your life more consistently with your values and philosophy and take greater pride in your accomplishments.

• **Seek allies against self-doubt.** You'll learn how to create a community of support—allies against self-doubt who are by your side—and surround yourself with people who acknowledge and value your victories and achievements.

I have great respect for your wisdom and courage as you make your way through your twenties. I am also keenly aware of your competence and basic common sense—even when you might not be able to recognize your own special skills and talents. Over the years, I have learned a great many things from the young women I have worked with, and this book reflects their knowledge and insights as much as mine.

As we begin to challenge together the expectations that create the pressures in your life, you too will find that you are able to make decisions based on what you really want, not on what you think society wants from you. By saying no to self-doubt, you will begin to define your life in your own terms, and realize that what might feel like pressures and expectations are, in reality, wonderful options and opportunities.

CHAPTER ONE

Get a Man

"MEETING AND MARRYING the man of my dreams is something I've wanted for as long as I can remember," says Dana, a twenty-seven-year-old teacher from Chicago. "But lately the pressure has been getting to me. My best friend just got engaged, and I'm already afraid I won't have a date to bring to her wedding."

Getting a Man is the oldest and most basic expectation for a woman. When your mother was your age, it was the only objective she had to worry about. Even if she had a job, in most cases her work wasn't considered necessary. Now, a woman is expected to connect with a partner she can love and cherish as well as succeed independently in other areas of her life.

No wonder you're feeling confused and maybe even overwhelmed as you try to balance everything: It may seem that as soon as you get one of the many balls you're juggling to stop bouncing around, every other ball falls to the floor. You're most likely not the only one feeling this way. Talk with your friends and you'll find that many of them are going through similar experiences.

THE DILEMMA

"I can't seem to get it right," says Tori, a twenty-six-year-old assistant hotel manager from New Orleans. "I meet a guy I like and I start to think he's going to be the 'one.' Then for some reason it doesn't work out. I'm beginning to wonder if it's me—maybe I'm too high maintenance or I'm not pretty enough or smart enough or thin enough or *something*. Lately, I find myself doubting that I'll ever even have a serious boyfriend, never mind get married. It gets me really upset and makes me feel very insecure."

Do Tori's fears sound familiar? There are many different reasons why you and other women in their twenties continue to experience pressure to "Get a Man"—everything from a deep longing to be married or be in an intimate relationship, to a belief that marriage will gain you approval and legitimacy, to a fear of loneliness. The magazines that you read, the music you listen to, the TV sitcoms and movies you see remind you over and over again that without "someone" in your life, you will be incomplete.

There is also the additional pressure to start thinking about having children one day and figuring out how being a mother will fit into your future plans. "These days the independence that seemed so fabulous—at least to those of us who tend to use that word a lot—doesn't anymore," writes twenty-eight-year-old

Vanessa Grigoriadis in a *New York* magazine article "Baby Panic." Citing research by author Sylvia Ann Hewlett from her book *Creating a Life: Professional Women and the Quest for Children* that finds putting off having a child reduces a woman's chance of conceiving and getting pregnant, Ms. Grigoriadis concludes that "single motherhood, adoption, and any number of other solutions to the problem at hand are all workable, but let's be honest, they're not the first choice. Once again, we're put in the position of wanting—needing?—to look for what our mother referred to as 'husband material.' "

The idea that a woman can only be happy if she is in a relationship with a man starts very early—as early as during middle-school years, if not before. Katie, who is at the top of her seventh grade class, recently told me, "If I don't have a boyfriend, I'm nothing!"

In her landmark book *In a Different Voice,* Carol Gilligan observes how girls in early adolescence begin to lose connection with themselves in favor of a relationship with other people. The pressure to Get a Man is different for a teenager who still lives at home and is cared for by others, however, because a young girl is not expected to be looking for an eventual mate and life partner at this time in her life.

Not so for a twentysomething woman out on her own. The message you hear is loud and clear: If for some reason you find yourself alone or aren't sure you are ready to commit to a relationship, something must be wrong with you. If you accept this message without questioning it, you'll find yourself second-guessing your own judgment and intuition. The uncertainty that follows can get you to feel confused and paralyzed with indecision.

"Twentysomethings have high expectations," says Michael Stoller, president of Stoller Coaching in Chicago, in an interview with the *Honolulu Advertiser*. "Parents, teachers, friends all influence those expectations. You should have kids by thirty and be established in your career. Who said that? Is that something you really believe in? They put expectations on themselves and when you really get down to the core of it, they don't even realize why they made those expectations."

So what is the core of it? It's not that women "make" these expectations; these expectations, which are often invisible and insidious, are a part of the twenty-first century and influence all of us. The expectation that you will eventually marry and have children is one you will probably successfully and happily fulfill: For most women, this is a "supposed-to" that is also a very real and desired "want-to." The trick, then, is to distinguish what you want to do from what you think you "should" be doing. A good place to start is to keep in mind this statement: *Expectations create pressure, which then creates self-doubt.*

Let's see how three different women in their twenties— Dana, Elaine, and Jenny—face the pressure created by the expectation to Get a Man. We'll follow them as they go about resolving the dilemma of self-doubt in their lives by engaging in these four steps:

1. Recognize and name the problem.

2. Understand and challenge the expectation.

3. Connect to what you value and believe.

4. Seek allies against self-doubt.

MARRIAGE AND MOTHERHOOD

For as long as Dana can remember, she has dreamed of getting married and having children. Dana comes from a large family and knows what growing up in a big household is like; she welcomes the feelings of security and companionship she believes a husband and children will offer. For Dana, Getting a Man doesn't really feel like an expectation—she knows what she wants.

Dana dated in college but none of her relationships turned out to be serious. Her friends used to make fun of her that her rules for keeping a boyfriend for more than a couple of months were very specific: He had to be interested in commitment and marriage. Her friends would tease her that she probably wasn't going to find a husband among her party crowd, and they would wonder why the rush.

But Dana continued to long for her own home and family. And a career, of course. After college, she went on to graduate school and got her master's degree in education. Even there, she felt different from her classmates. Marriage and babies were the furthest thing from their minds. What was wrong with her? Was she afraid to strike out on her own? Could she only feel complete if she were with a man? Was she trying to recreate her parents' marriage?

Now twenty-seven, Dana teaches fifth grade in an inner-city school in Chicago. Although she is extremely successful—she was recently named Teacher of the Year in her district—Dana is discouraged because she still hasn't met the "right" man. Lately, she finds herself wondering if getting married is what she really wants after all. She also finds herself making excuses for why she hasn't met someone yet.

"I'm not dating that much now because all the guys I meet seem really spooked by the idea of marriage," she says. "Maybe I come on too strong or my standards are too high. Some of my friends are already engaged so it could also mean that I'm not meant to get married."

The more discouraged Dana becomes, the more she finds herself questioning her true motives for getting married in the first place. Soon she can't distinguish between her own desire to be in a meaningful relationship that might lead to something permanent and what feels like the pressure to do so.

Just when Dana is about to give up finding her ideal man, she meets Jason at a jazz concert. He's cute, smart, funny, easy to be with, and what's more, he is definitely attracted to her. "This is it," she decides.

Dana doesn't let herself consider whether or not Jason is someone she wants to be with for the rest of her life. The expectation to Get a Man has swamped her desire to be with someone. Dana stops asking herself if Jason is the kind of man she would want for her husband and father to her children: The only question that concerns her now is, "Does he like me?" She doesn't ask, "Do I like him?"

Increasingly, Dana finds herself becoming overly concerned about how she looks, and works out whenever she can even though she has precious little time during the day. She starts obsessing about Jason's responses, lack of responses, what he says or doesn't say. She worries when he doesn't return her calls right away or answer her e-mails for a couple of hours.

Self-doubt and insecurity begin to define Dana's relationship with Jason. She becomes unclear about what she truly wants and gradually finds she is unable to remember, let alone attend to her own needs. As Dana becomes more and more immersed in her relationship with Jason, she feels increasingly "disconnected" from herself—not only from what she wants but also from who she is. She doesn't like how this is affecting her: She finds herself losing patience with her students, snapping at her mother, checking her weight several times a day.

"I can't even remember what's important to me anymore," Dana says. "I don't know what I want or don't want."

Dana is in a maze and needs to find her way out. Why is she feeling so clouded by self-doubt and insecurity in her relationship with Jason? Dana thinks it's her fault, that she is not an adequate partner for Jason. She worries that she isn't available enough to him both emotionally and sexually when they spend time together. That she comes across as too needy.

"I find myself constantly checking to make sure I'm doing the right thing," she explains. "I never know if Jason likes what I'm doing or is turned off by it. Whenever something goes wrong with us, I just think it's my fault."

Dana usually gets a phone call or e-mail from Jason every day. One day when she doesn't hear from him, she begins to think that she has done something wrong. She starts to obsess about what it might be. She tries to remember their last communication with each other. What did she say? What did he say? Then she wonders if she should phone him. What would he think if she did? Would he accuse her of checking up on him?

If Dana is to determine what's really going on, it would be helpful for her to start paying attention to when she begins to feel so confused and upset. Now she is so overwhelmed by the problem that she has lost touch, not only with what she wants but also with who she is. By focusing on what is happening to her, she can begin to think about what the problem may be.

I suggest that Dana name the problem in a way that makes

sense to her. She decides to call it "insecurity" and "self-doubt"—she doesn't really know where she stands with Jason. I explain that by her giving what she feels a specific name, she can use it to describe her experiences.

The act of noticing the problem allows Dana to take a step away from how it is affecting her. She begins to see that insecurity is influencing many different aspects of her life: She's avoiding food, drinking too much, neglecting herself, losing her temper, and thinking of herself as a failure. It doesn't take long for Dana to realize she dislikes what the problem is doing to her.

Dana wants to make a different decision about her relationship with Jason, one that is not clouded by insecurity or self-doubt. By exposing the problem, she is already experiencing some freedom from it and is in a stronger position to see how much it has influenced her life in a way she doesn't like.

"It has been so long since someone actually wanted to be with me that I thought Jason was my dream come true," Dana says. "I wanted to get married so badly that I stopped thinking about whether I really wanted Jason as my partner. I just told myself I was supposed to be on this path. Now, I'm beginning to understand that I don't have to be with him if I don't want to. I can think about whether or not we fit together or if I'm just caught up in the pressure to get married."

Dana is creating her own road map by acting from self-confidence, not self-doubt. She is also reconnecting with her desire to be married and have a family, at the same time realizing that she doesn't have to just settle for whomever comes along or pays attention to her. Dana eventually decides that her relationship with Jason isn't working for her, that she would rather be alone for a while until she meets a man who is right for her.

By successfully clearing away self-doubt, Dana can see what is bothering her about her relationship with Jason. She becomes more relaxed in her life and more at ease with what she wants. She also finds it much easier to meet people and enjoy their company.

I encourage Dana to talk about how she is overcoming self-doubt with others. Dana decides to share her thoughts and experiences with some close friends from her school. She also has long conversations with her mother, who has supported her throughout this difficult relationship with Jason. Dana talks about what she wants from her life, and her mother encourages her to keep looking for the person who will be "right" for her.

Several months later, Dana meets Shawn at a friend's party. He's also a teacher and shares her desire to settle down and start a family. They eventually start dating and find they fit together well.

"I like the way I am with him," Dana says. "I'm more confident, secure, and strong. It feels great!"

It is still early in the relationship, but Dana and Shawn are talking about their future together and have made plans to visit their respective families together during the holidays.

A SPACE OF HER OWN

Elaine, twenty-nine, has been in a relationship with Doug for three years. He wants to get married too, or at least that's what she thought when they first got together. They eventually split up but have never really stopped seeing each other. When Elaine moves to Atlanta to take a job with a catering company, Doug decides to join her there.

Elaine keeps having a nagging thought: "Maybe my relationship with Doug isn't right. Maybe we're too intertwined. Sometimes it feels as if I don't have any space. What if I don't ever have the chance to travel by myself like I've always wanted to?"

Elaine is not ready, however, to think about planning a trip for herself. Her first priority is making sure that everything is okay between her and Doug. Elaine finds she has a difficult time taking care of her own needs and the relationship at the same time. More and more, she "over-attends" to Doug, whether or not he even seems interested in her attention and concern.

The pressure to keep a man is clouding Elaine's ability to recognize her own wants and needs. This then leads to Elaine questioning if she has to leave Doug so she can create the space of her own she so desperately wants.

"One of the big things that's holding me back is my desire to have children," Elaine explains. "If I broke up with Doug now, I would be that much older before I could even start to think about having a baby. Let's say I meet a man right away. I would still want to get to know him for two years before we get married—by then, I'd be thirty-one. The pressure feels enormous."

Elaine is becoming more and more consumed by her desire to be in a relationship and have children; she's afraid she has stopped listening to her intuition, which continues to remind her of her need for space. When Elaine gets an opportunity to take a trip to Italy for three weeks, she decides to use it as an opportunity to break off her relationship with Doug. She will now be free to take the journey she's always yearned for.

The trip is everything Elaine dreams of. She feels confident and sure of herself. She loves Italy and loves learning new cooking ideas and techniques. Soon after returning home, however, Elaine gets a job in a trendy new restaurant and finds herself once again seriously involved in a new relationship. Even though she's crazy about Steve, the sous-chef at the restaurant, it turns out they are experiencing some of the same difficulties she had with Doug. Once again Elaine finds herself "over-attending" to Steve's needs at the expense of her own. The familiar nagging feeling that she is losing the connection to her own space is starting to creep back in.

When I ask Elaine to describe what she means by "space," she says that it's not just a geographic or physical concept; space also has to do with creating room for herself, time of her own, and pursuing her own interests and desires. Now Elaine is more confused than ever: She knows what she needs to do, but she just doesn't know how to do it. And time is short. What about the family she wants? She can't wait much longer. And what about space then? With kids it will be much more difficult.

Elaine knows she doesn't want to go through the same problem over and over. When I ask her to name the problem, she calls it "lack of trust" or "self-doubt." This lack of trust in her own knowledge is making her unsure about what she knows: Sometimes she wants to be with Steve, other times she wants to be on her own.

"What happens if my relationship with Steve turns out to be a replay of the one I had with Doug?" she asks. "Maybe I'm going on automatic, just to have a man in my life."

Elaine begins to notice how the lack of trust in her own intuition is influencing her life. She realizes she wants no more of it. She listened to herself when she broke off with Doug and took her long desired journey to Italy. How can she reconnect once again to what she truly wants?

I ask Elaine what taking the trip to Italy means to her. She describes returning from Europe and walking right into a ready-made relationship with Steve. The pressure to Get a Man had overridden her recent experience of creating her own space; no sooner had she stepped off the plane than the expectation hit her once again with full force. In addition, now that she was back home in her familiar surroundings, she found herself more vulnerable to those earlier feelings of self-doubt that were so much a part of her relationship with Doug.

Elaine wants to strike a balance between being in a relationship with Steve and having her own space. As she begins to identify the pressure she's feeling, she can make a distinction between what she wants for herself—to be in a relationship and have children—and how the pressure is clouding her thinking and judgment. Elaine begins to reconnect with her knowledge that space means having your own life, even if you're in a relationship.

Elaine remembers that when she was growing up, it was important for her to have a life separate from her alcoholic father and her mother who seemed caught in the relationship with him. Elaine wants nothing of that and knows it; she also knows that her survival now depends on her defining a life for herself in the context of creating her own family. She believes she is ready to do that too.

Elaine decides to stay in the relationship with Steve, but only by going to couples therapy together and mapping out a relationship that works for both of them. She begins to share her thinking and concerns with Steve, and finds that he is willing to support her in continuing to create a space of her own. They are making wedding plans and want to get pregnant in the near future so they can start the family they both so clearly desire.

It's helpful to reconnect with past moments of success, and remember those persons who may have noticed your competence and acted as your allies. When I ask Elaine to think about a person in her past who would not be surprised at the positive steps she is now taking, she immediately says it would be her grandmother.

"Even when I was little, my grandmother praised me for my independent spirit," Elaine recalls. "If she were here now, she'd say, 'I'm so proud of you, baby. I'm so proud!' "

The answers to our future are often hidden in the past. Once Elaine is able to separate from self-doubt and lack of trust, she can face the expectation to Get a Man and remember the people and the moments in her past that feel right for her. Then she can— and does—move forward in her life.

COMPANIONSHIP AND INTIMACY

Jenny is terrified she will end up alone. At twenty-five, she wants to be in an intimate relationship, but her fear of loneliness looms so large that sometimes she finds it difficult to be certain about what she really wants.

Jenny met Lela in her senior year at the University of Wisconsin at one of the gay-lesbian meetings on campus. Jenny was living in a rented room near school and feeling more alone than at any other time in her life. Her decision to move in with Lela was a no-brainer; they started living together almost immediately.

From the beginning, Jenny knows it's all wrong. Lela is jealous of her other friends and possessive of how she spends her time. Yet, even though the relationship with Lela continually makes her feel bad, Jenny can't bear to think of being alone again. She desperately longs for companionship and intimacy, and feels compelled to work things out with Lela.

As the pressure to be with someone becomes more and more overwhelming, Jenny begins to doubt her own feelings and intuition, blaming her own shortcomings for the problems with Lela. She assumes she must be doing something wrong, so she stops seeing her friends and spends virtually all of her free time with Lela. This only makes Jenny even more unhappy and lonelier than before.

The expectation to be with someone has taken over Jenny's life. She can no longer tell if she really wants to be with Lela or is just going through the motions to avoid being alone. She starts to question whether or not she wants to be with a woman at all. Earlier on in college Jenny had been involved in a relationship with a man, but knew in her heart that she "liked girls." However, she also felt she should be with Nick because that's what she was "supposed to" do.

Now, even though Jenny is with a woman, the relationship with Lela is beginning to feel wrong in the same ways it had with Nick. She's lonely, isolated, has fallen out of touch with her friends, and doubts that other people like her. Jenny used to assume it was her relationship with a man that had made her feel bad because it wasn't what she truly wanted. But now with Lela it feels just as bad. She is trapped and unable to find a way to extricate herself even though she knows she needs to.

Fear has gotten Jenny into a relationship and fear is keeping her there. She is not paying attention to what her heart is telling her: that being with Lela is not right for her.

"I guess I've always known on some level that the relationship was wrong," Jenny says. "But now I don't know what I want. I'm doubting myself and becoming more and more confused."

Jenny is blinded to whatever options may exist for her. In order to create a road map that will lead her out of her dilemma of self-doubt, she needs to get some freedom from the problem. Jenny begins by naming the problem as "feeling wrong." She tries to recognize what triggers "feeling wrong" and all the ways it gets to her.

I suggest that Jenny write down in a journal how the problem is affecting her. Jenny reads the list: "The problem—or 'feeling wrong'—creates a knot in my stomach and a tightness in my throat. I have recurring ideas in my head that I've made bad choices. I think I'm a bad person."

Jenny is paying attention to the emotions that accompany her "feeling wrong"—the anger, sadness, and deep despair. And she hates the feeling.

"I so want to get away from it," she says. "I know that I have to decide between changing my living situation and separating from Lela, or changing how I'm feeling and then seeing if I can work out the difficulties we're having."

As Jenny notices how the pressure to be with someone is influencing her to feel wrong and doubt herself, she remembers the loneliness she endured during her last year of college. She recalls some of the pressures she experienced during that time— her brother's car accident, the upcoming graduation, her senior thesis—and how difficult it had been to have time for an active social life.

Jenny finds herself beginning to distinguish her loneliness from how she feels now in the relationship with Lela. Lately, she's been feeling disconnected from so many of the things she likes to do. She has given up rock climbing and river rafting, stopped going to museums and art galleries, and hasn't called her old friends in ages. She is lonely in a different way, and it's becoming clearer that she doesn't want to be in a relationship where she can't be herself.

"How did this happen to me?" Jenny wonders. "Maybe the fear of loneliness pushed me to pursue a relationship as the 'answer' to all my problems. Where did I ever get that idea?"

Jenny also questions the pressure that society puts on women to partner up. Maybe the relationship with Lela isn't about a sexual-identity problem after all; maybe it is just not the right relationship for her. Jenny decides she wants to continue in her quest for a woman partner in her life; just because she and Lela aren't right for each other doesn't mean something is wrong with her or with what she wants to do.

The expectation to be with someone has pressured Jenny into partnering, then gets her to feel wrong about her choices. Once Jenny begins to make the connection between feeling wrong and partnering as the solution to loneliness, she can see that she's able to resist the pressure to make a relationship work out no matter what, even if it isn't right for her. Jenny is then in a position to start thinking about what she really wants in her life.

As Jenny faces the fear that is keeping her with Lela, she realizes that the expectation to Get a Man isn't the problem after all. As a matter of fact, she doesn't want to be subjected to any expectation, including Get a Woman. Now she can start distinguishing between the loneliness she feels in her life and the loneliness that comes with "feeling wrong" in a relationship.

Jenny is on the path to making some important distinctions between her own preferences and the expectations that society has for her. She sees that she can challenge this expectation by being comfortable with who she is as a person, whether alone or with a partner.

"It isn't about Lela," Jenny says. "It isn't even about the relationship or about me. It's about being expected to do something and feeling wrong if it's not going the way you think it should."

Jenny eventually decides to end her relationship with Lela and makes plans to lead an adventure tour to New Zealand with her kayaking group. She calls her old friends and plans a going-away party with them to celebrate her new life, free from the old life of "feeling wrong" and "fear of loneliness." She is ready to make her own decisions and define her own life. On the trip, Jenny finds herself much freer to make new friends without the pressure to meet someone special. She knows that eventually she'll connect with the right person for her.

WHAT CAN YOU DO?

Like Dana, Elaine, and Jenny, you also probably feel the pressure from the expectation to Get a Man or be with someone. Most women do. This pressure can lead to self-doubt, which can color your thinking and confuse you.

Think about how you are being influenced by the expectation to Get a Man. You might be in a relationship now or by yourself; you might want to be with someone or are unsure about whether the person you're currently involved with is right for you. Whatever your situation is, something might be bothering you but you don't know exactly what. You may feel uncertain, confused, or discouraged. You might second-guess yourself, feel insecure, or have an overall sense of negativity.

Dana is convinced she knows what she wants—marriage and children—but somewhere along the line it all becomes unclear. She finds herself unable to remember, let alone take care of her own needs when she is with Jason, and becomes increasingly disconnected from what she wants to do and even who she is. Elaine is once again "over-attending" to a boyfriend's needs at the expense of her own: The familiar nagging feeling that she's losing her own space is starting to create anxiety. Jenny also begins to doubt her own feelings and intuition in her relationship with Lela. She blames her own shortcomings for the problems between them, and assumes that she is at fault.

Does any of this sound familiar? Ask yourself the following questions:

- If you are in a relationship, and something is worrying or bothering you, how would you describe this worry?

- If you are not in a relationship, what concerns do you have about not being in one?

- If you are lonely, how do you think a relationship will take care of your problem?

- If you are attracted to women and are uncertain about it, what are you feeling about that?

Sometimes the problem isn't so clear-cut—it's more that something just doesn't seem "right." As you can see with Dana, Elaine, and Jenny, however, there are ways to figure out what's happening to you and create a road map to help you make your way through your twenties with confidence.

RECOGNIZE AND NAME THE PROBLEM

The first step in challenging the expectations in your life is to name the problem. Dana calls it "insecurity"; Elaine describes it as "lack of trust"; and Jenny says it is "feeling wrong." Each woman sees the problem as some form of "self-doubt," and naming it allows her to refer back to it and describe what it is doing to her. This, in turn, allows her to feel some freedom from it.

Perhaps you're overwhelmed, or you know something is wrong but you don't know exactly what it is. Take a step away from what you're feeling and notice what is happening to you. Be as specific as possible. You might call what is going on "fear" or "self-blame" or "second-guessing." You might choose one of the names that Dana or Elaine or Jenny use. Whatever name you select, however, it has to fit for you.

Now, observe when the problem occurs and what triggers it. Dana notices that the slightest event can create "insecurity" for her; for example, not hearing from Jason for a day or two or a girlfriend neglecting to ask her what she was doing for the weekend. As Dana begins to notice the triggers that set off the "insecurity," she can recognize the problem and not feel so bad about herself.

How does the problem you've named affect you? Dana sees that "insecurity" and "self-doubt" influence her eating and drinking habits, make her more irritable, and get her to believe she's a failure. Elaine thinks "lack of trust" and "self-doubt" make her confused about what she wants, and lead her to "over-attend" to her partner's needs at the expense of her own. Jenny knows all too well that "feeling wrong" has physical repercussions: a knot in her stomach and tightness in her throat. It also gives her the idea that she has made bad choices and is even a bad person.

What ideas end up in your head? Are you affected physically? What actions do you find yourself taking that might not be helpful? When do you feel bad about yourself?

Begin by paying attention to all the ways the problem affects you and increases the pressure you're experiencing from the expectation to Get a Man:

- What messages does it send you about your current relationship?

- How does it get you to think about your future plans for getting married and having children?

- Does it make you feel something is wrong with you if you're alone?

- What specific ways does it affect your social life?

Once you can see all the ways that self-doubt (or insecurities or fear or feeling wrong) affect your thinking, feeling, and very being, then you will be close to making the decision that you want no part of the problem in your life.

How did Dana, Elaine, and Jenny go about freeing themselves from the influence of whatever the problem was for them? Dana doesn't like what "insecurity" and "self-doubt" are doing to her; she realizes it has clouded her desire to be a wife and mother. Elaine notices how "self-doubt" and "lack of trust" is keeping her from paying attention to what she already knows—that creating space for herself was important to her. Jenny hates "feeling wrong" and begins to doubt her sexual identity. Each woman clearly decides that she no longer wants "self-doubt" or one of its many versions to influence her decisions about being—or not being—with someone she cares for as well as her eventual plans for marriage, children, or a committed relationship.

By saying to yourself, "I don't want this negative influence in my life," you will be more in touch with what is happening to you. You will also be ready to take the next step and question why you're having this experience in the first place.

Have you ever wondered where your thoughts about the expectation to Get a Man are coming from? Because most of us don't question our thinking, we take our thoughts for granted. Or we second-guess ourselves, wondering what's so wrong with us that we can't Get a Man. To understand how to question your thinking, ask yourself: Why do I feel the pressure to Get a Man? Why can't I get a man? What do I really want?

Then ask: What am I thinking? Where did I get that idea? What does it really mean?

It's hard enough to know what you are thinking, let alone ask yourself what it means. When you begin to question yourself from a different perspective, it allows you to be thoughtful about the choices and decisions you make.

To help you understand how you think about the pressure from this first expectation, start by reviewing your relationships. You may prefer to respond to these questions with a friend or by writing your answers in a journal.

- Why am I with this person?

- What are some of the reasons that our relationship is working out?

- Am I thinking more about if I like this person or about whether or not this person likes me?

As you look over your answers, you may see that the pressure to be involved in a committed relationship is influencing your life more than you think—and certainly more than you want. Dana realizes she desired marriage so intensely that she lost sight of herself in finding a potential partner. Elaine understands the expectation to Get a Man overrode her important need to create her own space. Jenny recognizes that she needs to face the loneliness that she thought being with someone would fix.

As Dana, Elaine, and Jenny start to notice why they are making certain choices, they also come to realize that they are no longer just "doing" their lives. Once you see that your thoughts and actions are being influenced by the expectation to Get a Man, you too can meet this expectation and challenge it.

UNDERSTAND AND CHALLENGE THE EXPECTATION

Because the expectation for a woman to Get a Man is deeply embedded in an age-old injunction from many societies and cultures throughout the world, you probably don't experience it as a direct command or demand. Instead, you just "know" that you want to get married and have children. This expectation creates such pressure in your life that it's hard to challenge it until you first clear away the self-doubt. Once Dana, Elaine, and Jenny face their experience of self-doubt and realize they no longer want it in their lives, they can understand it is coming from the pressure of the expectation and begin to challenge it. And so can you.

When Dana realizes she has fallen victim to the expectation, she can say: "Now I'm beginning to understand that I don't have to be with Jason if I don't want to." She understands she has a choice and can think more clearly about what she wants. Ask yourself if you too are being overly influenced by this expectation or if you can understand the different options available to you.

Elaine pays attention to what is happening to her. She sees that she can create space for herself but that she is also vulnerable to the reemergence of self-doubt and the pressure of the expectation. She then realizes she wants to strike a balance between being in a relationship and having her own space. How can you pay attention to what is happening in your relationships from a place of security rather than one of self-doubt? Are you able to recognize where you might be vulnerable, but also realize what is important to you?

Jenny comes to see that she can leave a relationship that isn't right for her by making the connection between feeling wrong, loneliness, and partnering as a "solution." Once she is able to notice how the expectation has pressured her to make certain choices, she begins to move ahead in her life from a position of confidence, not fear. Can you resist the pressure of this expectation and make decisions from a place of confidence rather than from one of fear and loneliness?

Because Dana, Elaine, and Jenny are able to challenge the expectation to Get a Man, they can understand the choices they have and consider what they want in a relationship. They are able to notice if their current relationship is a "solution" or quick fix for some other problem, and then look for ways to resist the pressure if it is. By paying attention to where they might be vulnerable, each woman can realize what is important to her.

Challenging the expectation to Get a Man also means making distinctions. Ask yourself the following questions:

- Can I distinguish between what I want in a relationship and what the pressure to Get a Man makes me think I want?

- Does the relationship I'm in "fit" my standards?

- What are the reasons I got into this relationship?

- Why am I in staying in this relationship?

Your answers are part of the road map you are creating to help you make important distinctions between what you really want and what the expectation is making you "think" you want.

CONNECT TO WHAT YOU VALUE AND BELIEVE

Carol Gilligan writes about "connecting to your own voice," which is really connecting to what you know and to what you value and believe. By remembering the times you have been confident in the past, you will be able to reconnect with what you know about your talents and skills, as well as what you value and believe about yourself, your relationships, and your place in the world. You can then bring that knowledge and confidence into your present life. It's important to focus on times when you felt confident and competent, not just when others told you that you were. By connecting with your competence, you will get better at making distinctions between how the expectation to Get a Man affects you and what you know and believe about yourself and others. This will allow you to act from your own history of self-knowledge, rather than from fear or worry.

Dana reconnects with her long-standing desire to be married and have a family, realizing she doesn't have to settle for just anyone who comes along. Elaine remembers the importance of having her own space and reconnects to a growing-up experience where creating her own space was critical for survival. Jenny recalls how she could successfully challenge the fear of loneliness in the past, and begins to make choices based on this knowledge.

How can remembering important values and reconnecting to a past history of competence and confidence help you? The following questions may help you recall events that remind you that you are a person who can take care of herself.

- What do you remember about your past desires, actions, and goals when you felt confident and competent?

- What values and beliefs do you hold that allow you to be firm in your commitment to yourself?

- Think about those memories that give you a sense of certainty, security, or hopefulness. What did you know then that you may have forgotten now?

- When you reconnect with what you know about your unique talents and skills in the past, how does this create new possibilities for you in the present?

- What persons in your life may have been present at any of these past moments and would have recognized your competence, not only then, but now? Is it a relative (parent, aunt or uncle, grandparent, older sibling), someone who mentored you (teacher or coach), or perhaps a good friend? What do you know about this competence yourself?

- What would these persons say about you then, and now? How would what they say fit your own experience of yourself?

Once you begin to reflect on and acknowledge this history of your competence in detail, list all the techniques and tools that you already possess to create the kind of relationship you want and that "fits" you. Then you can make choices and take actions in the present from this place of competence.

Although Dana, Elaine, and Jenny are successfully challenging the expectation to Get a Man, their stories do not have "happily ever after" endings. Each woman still has to continue to pay attention to how self-doubt is affecting her, remember what she wants, stay connected to what she values and believes, and work at creating intimate relationships that fit for her.

SEEK ALLIES AGAINST SELF-DOUBT

Help is always at hand, and you are not alone as you navigate through your twenties. The anthropologist Barbara Myerhoff writes about a "special type of recollection" where one purposely calls to mind those persons who stand with you and who are your community of support, both in the past and in the present. These people are your "allies" against self-doubt.

The first ally on Dana's list is her mother, who supports her through her difficult relationship with Jason. Dana's allies also include her colleagues, who named her "Teacher of the Year." Elaine finds that Steve can be a support to her, and she clearly recalls her grandmother, no longer living but a part of her "virtual" community. Elaine knows her grandmother would be proud of her now, as she was when she was young. Jenny considers as allies her old friends who stayed with her even though her relationship with Lela had cut her off from them for some time.

What are the criteria for membership in your community of support? Each ally must have real knowledge of your competence and confidence in the path you choose. Your allies are those persons who believe in you, and witness how you act with confidence and seek to stay connected to your own knowledge.

Who are your allies?

Develop a list of specific times in your past when you were pleased about the decisions you made with regard to a relationship or had a sense of your own competence as a woman who could take care of herself as well as others.

- What were the specifics of each occasion?

- Who was present at those times?

- Who might have noticed your competence?

Who from your past—a teacher, a relative, one of your parents—would not be surprised at the competent ways in which you are now acting in challenging the pressure of the expectation to Get a Man?

- What did this person know about you then that would have predicted your current behavior?

- What would this person say about you now as they notice the resurgence of your confidence and competence to have the relationship you desire?

If these people are no longer living, think about how you can continue to keep them alive in your memory as they virtually support you in your efforts.

Not everyone can be an ally. Often people who are close to us say things—perhaps in their effort to help—that inadvertently feed self-doubt. Or some people are struggling with their own version of self-doubt, which clouds their thinking and makes their words seem less than supportive. You may need to help those who are currently in your life remain allies so they can encourage and support you as you resist the pressure from this expectation. Here are some clues for you to help others help you.

Helping your mother. Sometimes you may think your mother doesn't understand you. She may be so full of worry and fear for you that her concerns are all you hear. This, unfortunately, can make your experience of self-doubt even bigger. Imagine what it will be like when you have children: You will want them to think well of you as a mother. You will want them to know they can count on you, that you love them, would do anything for them, and would stand with them against whatever problems they have in their lives. Here are some ideas for how you can help your mother do this for you:

- Tell her about your efforts to overcome self-doubt.

- Let her know the important distinctions you are making between the pressure to follow the expectation—one that she may also know—and what you want in a relationship.

- Plan together what you might say to other relatives who ask: "So, anybody interesting in your life?" That way your mother can feel she's helping you not be too pressured by that question.

- Keep her posted on the decisions you are making about whom you want to be with and the choices you make that you are happy about.

- Let your mother know you like it when she says she's proud of you or pleased with your show of self-confidence.

WHAT CAN BE SAID?

YOUR MOTHER MIGHT SAY ABOUT YOU

- She's focusing on her career right now.

- We both talked about how important it is not to jump into just any relationship.

- She's not seeing anyone currently, and it's not a concern for either one of us.

YOU MIGHT SAY

- I'm just keeping my eyes open.

- Someone interesting could show up any day.

- I'm confident I'll meet someone when the time is right.

By keeping the lines of communication open between you and your mother, you will experience her not only on your side but also by your side.

Helping your women friends. Your friends also get discouraged, and when they hear your problems and the insecurity you're dealing with, it brings to mind their own struggles. Pretty soon you may find they don't want to be around you if the conversations are too painful. So, rather than getting together for a gripe session, think about what you would like to hear from a friend and what would feel supportive.

• Ask your friend if her experience is like yours. Does she have self-doubt, insecurity, fear of loneliness in her relationships? Assure her she's not the only one.

• Tell her about the successes you've had in fighting self-doubt (or fear or anxiety) in your relationship with your boyfriend or partner. Ask about her successes.

• Wonder aloud with her about the pressures to get married, have children, settle down, Get a Man.

• Celebrate the decisions about relationships you're pleased about.

• Do the exercises from this chapter together.

• Create a ceremony for challenging the expectation to Get a Man or be with someone, and invite your mothers and all your women friends to attend.

In order to build an even closer, more supportive ally group with friends, you can also notice the questions you ask each other about your relationships, the experiences you share about your boyfriends and significant others, and the excitement you experience when you describe getting to know someone intimately.

Helping the men in your life. Self-doubt sometimes seems more a woman's issue because men usually look to external factors to explain their problems while women tend to search within for answers. So, although women may appear totally self-assured and confident, internally we experience feelings of doubt about our talents and skills. When the men who love us and care about us—our fathers, boyfriends, brothers, and other male friends— hear about this self-doubt, it sometimes scares them; they think they must "fix" it. When they can't, they often feel inadequate and even incompetent.

To help the men in your life be your allies, let them know about your "wins." Tell them that their support and availability are important to you, and you value their encouragement. They want you to be successful too.

GOING FORWARD WITH COMPETENCE

Self-doubt is a recurring dilemma that can show up around any relationship, whether it's casual, semi-serious, or has a strong possibility for commitment. Being close with someone is a strong desire for most women. When any form of self-doubt gets you to question your desire and your goals, it undermines the core of your value system. By overcoming fear, insecurity, or worry and challenging the expectation that creates your experience, you can more clearly decide what kind of relationship works for you and whether or not you might want a particular person in your life. You'll then be ready to make a confident choice about whom you would like to share your life with.

CHAPTER TWO

Have a Career

MELISSA'S GOAL IS to be a television producer. "That's why I decided to attend UCLA," she explains. "But it's already been two years since I got a degree in film and television, and I'm beginning to question whether I really want a career in the entertainment industry after all. I've had a couple of interesting jobs but none that I really feel passionate about. I want to do something I can look forward to in the morning, something that has meaning and is important. Yet, the more I'm out there, the more I wonder if this is the kind of work I really want to devote my life to."

Today you have a far wider range of employment opportunities than any other generation of women. But, as Melissa is discovering, you not only have to *know* what you want to do but also feel personally fulfilled in accomplishing your goal. If you don't have passion for your work or aren't moving forward in your career as fast as you would like, you may question your skills, judgment, and even your desires. This second-guessing can create a spiral of uncertainty that may interfere with your power to decide clearly what kind of work you want or how to advance in your current job.

Many young women tell me stories of their mothers and grandmothers and their wonderful talents. These were talents that often went unfulfilled because the world of work was not as open to them. They were not expected to work, and their primary option was to stay at home and do their job as wife and mother. Today you can choose to fulfill your talents and follow your career dreams, an opportunity that is exciting, but can also be very scary.

THE DILEMMA

In the past, a woman worked not because she was supposed to—as women are today—but in order to supplement the family's income or because she had some extra time on her hands. Men had the "real" careers that gave them satisfaction and brought in money, while women were asked to devote their talents and energies toward raising their children and maintaining the home. Now, with more than 75 percent of American women in their twenties and early thirties holding down jobs, the option to "Have a Career" is a very real expectation.

The economic necessity of studying and training for a career is also a major factor for women in their twenties. Getting married no longer provides the once automatic guarantee that you will be taken care of and supported by your husband: The two-income family has become an accepted financial reality of American life. In addition, there's no established road map that you can follow as you try to fulfill your professional aspirations and dreams and perhaps raise a family as well.

You are most likely exploring new job possibilities on a regular basis as you search for a career you are committed to or work you feel passionate about. Although this can be challenging at times, it can also create great anxiety and stir up feelings of uncertainty. Your search for a perfect job is not unique, however. According to the U.S. Bureau of Labor Statistics, the average eighteen- to thirty-four-year-old holds 9.2 jobs during those years. A far cry from the past security of sticking to one job or one company—especially for a woman—for your entire professional career.

Lani, twenty-eight, works at a Philadelphia brokerage house. "Every time I think of leaving my job," she says, "I ask myself if it's a failure on my part or a genuine desire to get out of finance altogether and try something that will make me happier. Sometimes I don't know if the problem is with me or with the actual work here. What makes it even more confusing is that this is already my fourth job since college."

Like Lani, you too may find it difficult to distinguish between self-doubt and the reality of your work situation. Of course, finding a woman's way is not so clear in an environment still set up by men's rules. It's only recently that daughters as well as sons are expected—and prepared—to have a career, and the unwritten "training manuals" that describe how to manage in the streets and alleys of the workplace are still mostly unavailable to the women who are now trying to compete on an uneven playing field.

If you are like other women your age, you undoubtedly want

to have "something of your own," and see a career as "something that fulfills you." You want to make use of your talents, pursue your interests, do whatever gives your life meaning. You have so many alternatives, so many career choices, so many paths to try. You can even elect to stay home and raise your children at any point in your career, if you decide to do so.

Title VII of the 1964 Civil Rights Act created equal employment opportunity and opened the doors for women to enter the work world. But somewhere along the line, the wonderful "opportunity" for a woman to have a career became an unwritten requirement. You must work. You must excel at what you're doing. You must know what you want to do.

It's easy to understand why the different options available to a woman in her twenties can create such confusion. What happens if you have no idea what ignites your passion or where your talents lie? Or you do know and are finding some success in your job, but can't quite seem to understand what the rules of the workplace are? Or you want a job and a family, and are wondering how—and if—you can balance it all?

Like many young women I work with, you are most likely experiencing pressure from this second expectation in your life, to "Have a Career." This pressure, in turn, can open the door to a fear, or self-doubt, that sneaks into your life and affects you in subtle ways. You may feel uncertain and unclear about your professional choices and future plans. You may find yourself questioning your abilities and talents. You may wonder if you'll ever find meaning and satisfaction in your work. After a while, you may even begin to forget not only what you want to do but also who you are.

Happily, there are ways to clear your head and make the choices that are best for you.

1. Recognize and name the problem.

2. Understand and challenge the expectation.

3. Connect to what you value and believe.

4. Seek allies against self-doubt.

FINDING A PASSION

Melissa has always loved the arts, and left Denver to go to the University of California, Los Angeles so she could pursue a career in the entertainment industry. After college her plan was to find an entry-level job in a television production company that would eventually turn into full-time work. But now, at the age of twenty-four, Melissa is afraid she'll never find the job she dreamed of since she was in grade school. The two jobs she's had—one on an independent television pilot and the other as a set decorator on a music video—have not led to anything permanent. Melissa also realizes that in order for her to make it in the industry, she has to have connections or compromise her personal values in a way she just isn't willing to do. All in all, it's been a huge disappointment.

Melissa takes a job waitressing and continues with her writing and set design classes. But she's afraid that she is spinning her wheels. "What if I can't find a job that I really love?" she worries. "I know what I need to do but I just can't seem to make myself do it. I'm afraid that if I continue working at what I know to be dead-end jobs, I'll start to lose my passion entirely."

As upset as she is, it's a while before Melissa notices how much her job situation—or lack of it—is affecting every aspect of her life. She wakes up in the morning with an upset stomach and often can't eat. Instead of searching for another job, she lives on her tips and drops out of her classes. She is spending more and more time alone watching television. Her social life is nearly at a dead end and she is convinced that her friends no longer enjoy her company. And no wonder—she hardly likes being with herself either. She wonders if she should pack up and move home to Denver, even though that feels like a failure. Nothing seems right.

I ask Melissa to think about what she would call what is happening to her. At first, she says she doesn't know, maybe a low-grade depression or just feeling down. She knows she feels as if she's spinning out of control. When I ask her to tell me more about this "out-of-control" sensation, she says: "It makes me feel like something is really wrong with me, that somehow I've missed the boat. All my friends from college have successful careers and I'm still waiting tables."

Melissa talks about Andrea, who is running her own restaurant; Chip, who is a graphic designer at a high-tech company; and Amber, who just finished her Ph.D. in art history and has landed a teaching fellowship at Yale. "Not to mention my sisters," she adds. "They're both married with kids and careers. What's wrong with me?"

When I tell her that it sounds as if she's beginning to doubt herself, Melissa smiles. "*Beginning* to doubt myself?" she replies. "Are you kidding? Self-doubt is what I feel all the time."

Once Melissa begins to see self-doubt as the problem, I suggest that she notice some of the ways it affects her. One evening, as she's writing in her journal, she decides to list what self-doubt does to her on a daily basis. "I wake up in the morning with an upset feeling. I can't eat. I think about how much I hate my job but am afraid I don't know what else I want. I wonder about my friends who are engaged in interesting careers. I feel like a loser. I watch too much television. I don't even have the energy to look on the Internet for a job I might like better."

Even though this is a small step, it gives Melissa a sense of control. She is angry that self-doubt has taken over so many aspects of her life, and finds that this anger gives her more energy. Gradually, she begins to notice that her depression is starting to lift.

As Melissa frees herself, she starts to think more clearly. She realizes that ever since she can remember she has been feeling enormous pressure to know what she wanted to do, to have a career path, and to make her future happen. The expectation is huge. No wonder she had been so depressed. The idea that she was supposed to know what to do for the rest of her life was oppressive. She knows she should not let that expectation have so much power.

Melissa's mood feels lighter; she is less burdened by the pressure of the expectation to Have a Career. When her childhood friend Gina comes to town, they go to lunch and reminisce. Gina confides that she has always been in awe of Melissa's artistic talents, even when they were together in grade school.

"Remember when you wanted to be Dorothy in the school play, but I got the part?" Gina asks. "And then you stole the show as the Wicked Witch of the West?" Melissa laughs as their conversation opens the floodgate to countless other memories of what gave her pleasure in the past. She not only recalls her role in *The Wizard of Oz* but also pictures herself when she starred as Helena in *A Midsummer Night's Dream* during her sophomore year of high school. She then remembers how she loves to write, and how her short story won third prize in a statewide competition.

"I am happier when I'm doing something creative," Melissa tells Gina. "I think I'll enroll in acting classes and start to take my writing more seriously."

Melissa used to search the Internet for interesting jobs but had never actually been able to bring herself to apply for anything. "I always thought I wasn't qualified, that no one would want me," she explains. Now, after her talk with Gina, Melissa finds a listing on Monster.com for a job with a local magazine geared toward newcomers and visitors to the Los Angeles area. The editors are looking for someone to write descriptions of neighborhood restaurants, cafes, stores, as well as various services readers may be looking for. Without giving self-doubt a chance to even tweak her into hesitating, Melissa sends off her résumé with a sample of her writing.

Melissa is called in for an interview. Even though she doesn't know if she will get the job, she decides to have an impromptu dinner party to celebrate the return of her confidence and her growing victory over self-doubt. She invites those friends who have supported her even at her lowest point when she felt the most insecure.

After Melissa and her guests finish her famous homemade chocolate mousse, her friend Gina makes a toast: "To the new and secure Melissa," she says, adding, "I'm sorry if I've sounded unsympathetic in the past, but part of me was afraid that I might start becoming worried like Melissa. After all, sometimes it feels as if I'm just barely hanging in there."

Through the laughter and knowing nods, Melissa's friend Emma raises her glass for another toast. "My problem was that I was scared that Melissa's doubts would make me feel more insecure than I already do."

Melissa is on her way to challenging the expectation that she should have had her career together by now. While waiting to hear from the magazine editor, she goes back on-line and finds four other jobs that also sound interesting. She sends over her résumé and writing samples to each one without giving it a second thought. She also calls home and tells her parents that she misses them but has decided that Los Angeles is the place for her. She knows they'll be relived that she's happier about her life.

Melissa is starting to feel she has options and work possibilities on the horizon. She continues with her acting classes and waitressing job. She's more confident that her career will take off, enjoys her friends, and feels she has something to look forward to every day.

BEING SEEN

Amy, twenty-seven, got a job right out of college in sales for a prestigious high-tech firm. She moved to Boston after attending Carnegie Mellon when things were booming in the tech industry. She is making more money than she could have imagined, enjoys her coworkers, and feels acknowledged for what she does. She was recently promoted to a management position as director of the company's New England marketing division.

Even though Amy believes she's on the fast track at work, she notices that the other division heads never ask her or the only other woman on the team to join them for lunch or drinks

after work. And during the management meetings, her suggestions are met with dead silence: It's almost as if she's invisible.
When she presents a sales plan that she's worked on for days,
it's discounted without a discussion. Amy can't get her voice
heard, and, as a result, is beginning to doubt she has something
to say.

Amy has always prided herself on her ability to get along
with almost anybody. But now her confidence is slowly starting
to erode. Before every meeting she thinks, "This time will be different. I'll just be more assertive." Nothing she does seems to
work: The other managers continue to shrug their shoulders at
her ideas and bypass her comments.

Soon self-doubt begins to take hold. Amy is hesitant at meetings, knowing that no matter what she says, she won't be listened
to. Her neck and shoulders became tight before every meeting.
Some days she can hardly move her head, and soon begins drinking to relax when she comes home from work. The tightness in
her body is a constant reminder of how upset she feels on a daily
basis.

When I ask Amy to name the problem, she immediately says
"anxiety," then quickly corrects herself. "Well, maybe I'm just
overly upset," she says. "I'm losing faith in myself." We agree to
call Amy's problem "lack of confidence" and "overly upset."

Amy begins to pay special attention to how tense she becomes
when she thinks about her career. It seemed so easy in the beginning, but the pressure to keep her energy up makes it hard to
know if this management position suits her. She notices how much
she has changed from the take-no-prisoners, confident young
woman she had been during her first few years at her job to the insecure, second-guessing person she's become. The problem is so

overwhelming that it starts to touch every aspect of her life, not just work: She finds herself unsure of her friendships, her dating possibilities, as well as her interest in flamenco dancing, which has always been her special social outlet.

Amy soon realizes her experience at work is dragging her down. She can't keep living this way. She starts focusing on where the "lack of confidence" shows up most intensely, and realizes it is when she feels disregarded and ignored. She starts to wonder what it really means to Have a Career. Maybe women aren't supposed to work so hard. Maybe that's why for centuries women have mainly stayed at home, doing what they're "good" at—being a wife and a mother.

Amy thinks about leaving her company. As she reviews how the last few weeks have gone, she becomes more aware how self-doubt has been influencing her. It has gotten her to question her job as well as her talents; it's made her insecure in her relationships. But the worst is that it has raised questions about her identity. She realizes how treacherous self-doubt is, and decides that quitting self-doubt is a better idea than quitting her job. She just isn't sure how to do it.

Thinking about quitting self-doubt helps Amy know that she could benefit from some feedback. She calls Suzanne, a friend from college who is working in another Boston high-tech firm. After listening to Amy's story, Suzanne asks her: "Do you think the fact that practically all of the other managers on your team are men means anything? Maybe you're trying to play a man's game, which could be your downfall. Even though women and men are supposed to have equal opportunity, the bottom line is that it's still men who run most businesses and make the rules."

Suzanne tells Amy what works for her. "Women are great at creating and nurturing relationships," she explains, "and we should tap into those special talents. Try focusing on your interpersonal and networking skills, and see what happens."

Listening to Suzanne, Amy realizes how much self-doubt has overwhelmed her: She had even forgotten she has interpersonal skills. To jog her memory, Suzanne reminds Amy how good she was at organizing social events for their college dorm, had been chosen by the dean to welcome the incoming freshman class, and was their year's liaison to the alumni office.

With this reminder of her past confidence and success, Amy can make plans in the present. She decides to seek out the advice of some women from her company—the vice president of public relations, the assistant director of international sales, the other division head who confides to her that she too feels passed over and ignored at management meetings.

The more Amy speaks with the other women in the firm, the less alone and isolated she feels. She runs her marketing ideas by her female colleagues, listens to their input, incorporates their language suggestions, and gratefully gives them credit for their help in the final draft of her report.

Amy discusses her sales plan—accompanied by written documentation—at the next management meeting. Because she had connected with Anika, her female colleague on the team, beforehand, she knows she'll have backup. Amy gives a forceful and eloquent presentation. Later that day, Anika stops by Amy's office and says, "Thanks for your presentation today. I know it was hard, and I'm really glad you asked for my help. What you did gives me courage to speak up more myself."

That night Amy goes to her flamenco dancing class after not having the energy to do so for months. The next day she calls

Suzanne and suggests that they find a way to celebrate "women's knowledge" and her triumphant management meeting. First, though, Amy wants to know one thing: How was Suzanne able to notice what Amy was unable to see? Didn't Suzanne ever have any doubts herself?

"Of course I have doubts," Suzanne answers. "And it's still a struggle. I used to have terrible panic attacks just before my own management meetings. But I was too ashamed to ask anyone for advice. I'm still embarrassed by how much anxiety I have, but listening to you helps me see that I'm not alone."

Amy begins to realize that once she moves away from self-doubt even a little, there is more space in her mind to listen to her intuition and judgment. She thinks about how tenuous self-confidence can be when you feel isolated and alone, and how important it is to reach out to others for help and support.

THE BALANCING ACT

Remember Elaine? When we left her she and Steve were thinking about getting married and starting a family. Now, they have set a wedding date, and Steve is talking about their opening a restaurant together in a trendy new area of Atlanta. His plan is that he would be the chef and she would be the general manager.

Elaine likes the idea but is worried how they can afford investing in such an expensive venture while starting a family at the same time. Steve knows that she wants to get pregnant right away: Is he even thinking about how she could manage a start-up business *and* take care of babies? Elaine is unsure if she would be able to balance having children and running a home with her responsibilities to a new restaurant. Would the business drain her energy away from being a good wife and mother? Or vice versa? Maybe Steve would want her to hire someone to take care of her children when she is at work, something she doesn't want to do.

The bottom line is that Elaine is afraid that she might end up agreeing to what Steve wants, not what she wants. She is also concerned that if they do work together, she'll find herself deferring to him and have a hard time making her voice heard. Even more important, what happens if she's not able to maintain her own personal space, which she just recently recaptured for herself?

Elaine has always enjoyed working in the food business. In high school, she worked as hostess at a local cafe. Then she worked for a catering company, and after her trip to Italy, became a waitress in one of Atlanta's talked-about restaurants. But now she finds herself wondering if her interest in food is only a hobby, not a "real" career. Elaine is so anxious about this issue that she is questioning her desire to have any career at all. Maybe she should devote her cooking skills exclusively to preparing nurturing and healthy meals for her husband and children!

Although the thought of owning a restaurant with Steve has a certain appeal, Elaine's doubts are making her feel ambivalent about actually committing herself to making this dream a reality. At this point, Elaine is unsure if opening a restaurant is Steve's dream or her own.

Elaine soon realizes that some form of self-doubt is beginning to creep back into her life, not only forcing her to question her possible choice of a career but also attacking her relationship with Steve. Elaine calls the problem "second-guessing." Because she's gone through the wrestling with expectations experience before, Elaine starts identifying how "second-guessing" is affecting her. She is short with Steve, sometimes not wanting to be with him, let alone talk to him. Her waitressing job is wearing on her and she is irritable with customers. She begins to hate food to the point where she is not eating well.

When I ask Elaine to key into how much "second-guessing" is affecting her, she laughs and says, "Too much!" What she knows for certain, though, is that she doesn't want this problem to continue to upset her. She is also clear that she knows the pressure she's experiencing from the expectation to Have a Career is not coming from Steve so much as it is coming from a larger place—society, the world. The mounting fear tells her she will be unable to balance a career and a family, and still have her own space.

Elaine begins to challenge how this expectation is creating pressure for her. She realizes she wants something for herself that she cares about, a passion that is hers and not necessarily shared with Steve. Although Elaine recalls her delight in learning culinary arts while she was in Italy, she knows that she doesn't want to work in a restaurant, even one she would own with Steve. She also knows that this is not her decision alone; before she and Steve get married they need to discuss the distinction between her career and being a wife and a mother.

Out of curiosity, Elaine decides to read the want ads and surf the Internet to look at jobs outside the food industry. Nothing captures her imagination; she wonders if at twenty-nine, she may be too old to start over. She begins to question if she has wasted the last ten years of her life pursuing work in a field that holds no future for her. Perhaps she should be a stay-at-home mom and leave it at that.

Elaine calls her friend Kate, who used to work with her in the catering company. "I'm really confused," she confides. "I don't know if my passion for cooking should be a career path or just something I do for fun? Maybe I should forget the whole thing."

Kate reassures her. "You've always had a flair for flavor," she says, "and you know what foods work together. It's fun to take what you do well and make a career out of it. Take me for example. My experience in catering helped me eventually find a great job in the wine industry. Follow your passion; the rest will come."

Kate's words help Elaine think about what used to be her dream: creating a specialized catering company. She realizes she could do this from home, and it could easily dovetail with Steve's restaurant. Elaine knows she and Steve need to discuss her idea, but at least she will be coming into the conversation with a specific plan, not with second-guessing. Once again Elaine thinks of her grandmother and how proud she would be that Elaine is working to define what she wants and create her own space.

WHAT CAN YOU DO?

The expectation to Have a Career probably affects you in many of the same ways it does Melissa, Amy, and Elaine. Like the expectation to Get a Man, this second expectation can create enormous pressure and lead to some form of self-doubt, such as Melissa's "feeling out of control," Amy's "lack of confidence," or Elaine's "second-guessing."

No matter how the pressure from the expectation to Have a Career affects you, it's important to consider all the ways it may enter your life. The pressure might feel like a doubting of yourself, a vague sensation that something is wrong, a feeling of being stuck, or just not knowing what you want to do with your life. However, just like the first expectation, there is a way out of this confusion.

Begin by asking yourself how you think the expectation to Have a Career influences you. Maybe you've recently graduated from college and are thinking about how your major will translate into the real world. Or you—and your parents—are wondering what you'll be able to do with a degree in anthropology after all. Perhaps you're working at an entry-level job and are frustrated that your work doesn't allow you to use your strongest skills and talents. Let's say you're lucky and have a great job, but are feeling powerless in the face of the politics of your workplace. Or you've landed a career-path position in your chosen profession but are starting to question if it's really what you want to do after all.

Whatever your situation, you may have an overall sense that something's not right. You may feel vaguely upset, bored, or like you're spinning your wheels. For example, Melissa is looking for passion in her work, yet her struggle to find a job she loves is leaving her drained and powerless. Amy is losing confidence in her management skills, although she began her career with the highest hopes and ambitions. Elaine is overwhelmed by the fear she won't be able to balance marriage and family with a career that is meaningful for her.

RECOGNIZE AND NAME THE PROBLEM

To begin, pay attention to all the different ways you feel some form of pressure about your work life and how this pressure

CAREER CRISIS?

- Do you find yourself wondering if your job/career/profession is really the one you want?

- Are you concerned that you're supposed to know what you want to do for the rest of your life and worried that you don't?

- Do you feel stuck in something that once felt right to you but no longer seems to be?

- Are you unsure how to combine a successful career with a committed relationship?

- Do you question if what you like to do is really career material?

If you answered yes to any of these questions, you are being affected by the expectation to Have a Career.

influences your judgment and actions. Notice the specific instances when you experience self-doubt and uncertainty about the direction of your career path. By noticing and naming the problem created by the pressure from the expectation to Have a Career, you are exposing the problem and thus reducing its power over you.

What name would you give to your experience? Be as specific as possible. Melissa calls the problem "spinning her wheels" and "out of control." Amy thinks of it as "lack of confidence" and "overly upset." Elaine names it "second-guessing." All see it as some form of self-doubt.

Next, be aware of when the problem occurs. There are many small events that can trigger a sense of insecurity or self-doubt, and if you pay attention, you can identify them as they occur. Then when the problem appears, see what it does to you. For example, what happens when you meet a former classmate who seems really happy at her job? Maybe you're like Melissa, who questions her abilities when comparing herself to friends who are successful in their careers. What's your experience when your boss overlooks your efforts at work? Amy initially thinks it's her own shortcomings, not office politics, for what seems like her failure to be recognized and heard in management meetings. Do you sometimes blame yourself when things go awry at work? Perhaps you identify with Elaine's fears that she will be unable to successfully pursue her career once she gets married.

Self-doubt, or whatever you name the problem, affects each of us in different ways. Sometimes there's a physical response: For Melissa, it creates nervousness and an upset stomach; for Amy, a tightness in the neck and shoulders. Other times our reactions are psychological: Amy finds herself losing confidence and pulling back at her job. The problem may also enter into your interpersonal relationships: Elaine is aware that she's cranky with Steve and losing her temper at work, but doesn't know what to do about it.

Ask yourself how the pressure created from this expectation has entered your life. It may be telling you that you're no good at what you do, that you've made bad choices, that you'll never find work that will provide meaning and passion in your life. The pressure might be taking away your energy, leaving you exhausted. You may find yourself obsessing about the need to find your passion and worrying what will happen to you if you don't.

Self-doubt is like a virus. It is contagious and attaches itself to whoever may be vulnerable at the time. The better you become at noticing its insidious influence, the more prepared you'll be to fight it off. Once you decide to quit self-doubt, you'll have more space in your mind to pay attention to your own intuition. And, as you continue to gain more clarity, you'll find yourself questioning how self-doubt got to be such a large part of your life in the first place.

You are now ready to escape self-doubt's power over you and are well on your way to understanding that the pressure you are experiencing comes from the expectation to Have a Career. You can then ask yourself:

- Why am I not happy in my work?

- What are my expectations about what "should" be happening in my career?

- Where did I get those ideas?

- How can I focus on what I really want in my work life?

Recognizing and naming the problem is the first step in the process of overcoming self-doubt; you can now begin to question the expectation that has created the pressure you feel about your work life. This is an important shift in your thinking, and will better help you to make decisions about your career from a position of strength, not insecurity.

UNDERSTAND AND CHALLENGE THE EXPECTATION

You will see that once you clear self-doubt from your life and get free of the pressure from this expectation, options and possibilities that previously seemed invisible will begin to pop up. You will notice you have choices, that you no longer have to fall prey to any "shoulds" or "supposed-tos" regarding the decisions you make about your work life.

Although the assumption that a woman must Have a Career is not an age-old expectation like getting a man, it is extremely powerful nonetheless. Men are more apt to define themselves by their work, and now women are also expected to do so. In addition, because it seems that society values a successful career as much—if not more—than the work of wife and mother, the pressure to find and follow a career path can create tremendous anxiety for most women.

Unfortunately, there are very few established professional game plans for the working woman today who wants to have a successful career, enjoy meaningful work, and take care of her family—usually all at the same time. As a result, many women are now finding it necessary to create new rules to compete in a work world previously dominated by men. They also are finding that networking with other women is critical for establishing important support systems in all areas, but particularly in professions that have been previously closed to women.

Here are some different ways for you to go about understanding and challenging the expectation to Have a Career:

• Notice how you think about the expectation once you are clear of self-doubt. Melissa sees that it has affected her since her high school years, and then realizes she can challenge it by saying: "No one should have to know what they want to do for the rest of their lives." How can you understand the effects of this expectation on you, and what would you do to counter them?

• Pay attention to what thoughts come to your mind about your current work. Like Amy, perhaps your career success came easily to you, so the expectation may be affecting you more in terms of how you respond to a professional setting that is governed by men's rules. Does the way you are operating in the workplace fit for you? Is there some way you might use your women's knowledge to challenge certain office politics or taken-for-granted ways of doing things at work?

• Distinguish between your priorities. Elaine sees that she does want a career, but one of her own making that will allow her to balance work with her desire to be a wife and a mother. How can you stay firm in your preferences and not let the expectation to Have a Career take you away from them?

As you begin to understand how the pressure of this expectation affects you and make distinctions between what it tells you and what you want for yourself, you will be able to make decisions because they fit you, not because they're expected of you. Consider specific examples in your answers to the following questions:

• What constitutes "meaning" or "passion" in your work? Are you doing what you really like, or working at something because you think you're supposed to like it?

• What are small passions and big passions? Does it help to notice the difference? What enjoyment do you get from what you do?

• What do you like about your work? What bothers you the most?

• What networking, interpersonal, and relationship-building skills ("women's knowledge") can you use to your advantage?

• Are you resisting doing something you really want because you're afraid of compromising your personal life?

• What other ways is the expectation to Have a Career influencing you to do what you think you "should" do rather than what works for you?

Share your answers with friends—you'll probably discover how similar your experiences are. In challenging the expectation to Have a Career and making important distinctions about your work life, you will then be able to connect to your own knowledge and talents.

CONNECT TO WHAT YOU VALUE AND BELIEVE

Self-doubt is deceptive—it can make us forget what we're good at and disconnect us from what we know about ourselves. As you release yourself from self-doubt and challenge the expectation to Have a Career, you will find that you can more readily recall your past triumphs and acknowledge your current successes. You will also be more free to connect to the talents and skills that are part of your personal history but have gone unnoticed and unattended since self-doubt moved into your life.

The key to reconnecting to what you know is to remember your past experiences of knowledge, competence, and confidence. But how do you go about recounting what you do well? As your mind is freed up to search for past episodes and experiences that give you pride, memories will likely pop up. Other people can also help you remember your past successes: parents, relatives, or friends whose recollections might be richer than yours because they were not interrupted or colored by self-doubt. It's important, however, that their memories fit with your own sense of past confidence.

Try recalling events in middle school or high school, or earlier, where you showed some special ability or talent. Once Melissa's memory is triggered by Gina's reminding her that she brought down the house as the Wicked Witch of the West, Melissa remembers that she had talent—and passion—for acting. Maybe you participated in clubs or sports or volunteer activities where your special skills were notable. Amy realizes that her gift for getting people together was greatly admired—and remembered—by her classmates from college. Perhaps you held a job that made you feel really sure of yourself. Kate's praise of Elaine's skills when they worked together in the catering company inspires Elaine to continue with a food-related career.

What history of your relationship to work/career/profession can you remember and reconnect with? Earlier, you were able to "name the problem." Can you name a specific talent, skill, or interest that matches your best version of yourself? Maybe it's your "way with words" or "gift for facilitating" or "creative flair." What name best fits your special talents?

As you refresh your memory with past incidents that highlight your skills, interests, and competencies, see how they fit the choices you are currently making. Ask yourself these questions:

- Is the job I'm doing a match for what I am good at?

- If my job isn't a match, is there something else I want to be exploring?

- Are there ways I can make my current situation enjoyable?

- What do I look forward to in my work?

- Am I willing to make certain sacrifices to make my job work better?

Melissa enrolls in acting classes because it reconnects her with what gave her pleasure growing up. She isn't specifically looking for a job as an actress but wants passion in her life and believes theater is a way to experience it. She also decides to take her interest in writing more seriously, which gives her the confidence to apply for several editorial jobs. Melissa successfully overcomes her insecurity, which she celebrates with others; success in a career will follow.

Amy is reminded of her great interpersonal skills, and reclaims that knowledge at her job. She begins to network at her workplace, asks her coworkers for advice, tests her ideas out with her supervisor, and seeks out the support of the other woman on the management team. She prepares herself for an important presentation in which she can showcase her "women's knowledge." Amy reconnects with her ability to move forward in her career because she vanquishes "lack of confidence."

Elaine acknowledges her desire for her own space and sees the possibility of a career separate from her job as wife and mother. She can now negotiate with Steve, and bring in her own ideas so they can compromise in a way that will work for both of them: They will do this balancing act together. Elaine's success over "second-guessing" opens the door for her to seek a career that is truly for herself.

Self-doubt is an unpredictable opponent: Just when you think it's gone for good, it may unexpectedly reappear in your life. Perhaps you're in the business world and reconnect with your desire to be a teacher. Self-doubt may tell you that this is not a real desire, that you're only running away from a current challenge. Or maybe you're working as a physician's assistant, and a friend casually wonders why you haven't gone to medical school. All of a sudden, you find yourself questioning the value of your current work.

It is especially important to identify self-doubt as the culprit in these instances of uncertainty, and once again challenge the expectation that is creating it. Then go on to reconnect with your history of competence, paying special attention to past memories of confidence and success.

Notice how you feel about your current work/career situation and ask yourself the following questions:

1. What are my specific talents and skills?

2. How am I using those talents and skills in my current job?

3. What "woman's knowledge" do I bring to my work?

- skill in relationships
- ability to see interpersonal patterns

- knowledge of how to help others work together
- appreciation of others' talents

Once you have identified the areas where you feel most confident, you may find it helpful to make notes about how you have used your skills to overcome difficulties or improve your work situation. Keep track of the important shifts you have made throughout your work history and the ways you have created passion in your life. Most important, give yourself credit for your success over self-doubt as well as for your learning and achievements. Then, you can validate your victory over self-doubt in your professional life by celebrating with people who support and acknowledge your accomplishments.

SEEK ALLIES AGAINST SELF-DOUBT

You don't have to fight self-doubt by yourself. As you face decisions about your current job situation and future career path, it's important to realize that you have a community of friends and relatives who are there to support you. What you must do is identify who they are, and invite them to be your companions as you stave off self-doubt and continue to pursue a fulfilling and satisfying profession.

A good way to begin this process is to tell others both about your struggle with self-doubt and any successes you have along the way. Melissa talks to Gina, Amy goes to Suzanne, and Elaine confides in Kate. You too can reach out to friends and family and tell them what you're going through. Celebrate your successes over self-doubt together, and toast your mutual accomplishments. Ask them how self-doubt enters into their relationship with the workplace, and share with each other tips and techniques for dealing with the pressure of the expectation to Have a Career. (There are organizations, books, and Web sites to help you with this. See "Resources," p. 231.)

Perhaps there are older and more experienced women in your field whom you could ask to mentor you. Their perspective can be very helpful and their experiences may give you new insights and understanding.

It is important to remember, however, that sometimes those people who are closest to you need your help in learning how to support you as you make decisions regarding your career. They too may have been influenced by doubt as they notice your struggle, and would be relieved to hear your suggestions about what constitutes support for you. Here are some ways you can help them help you.

Helping your mother. Mothers often worry about their daughters and sometimes this concern comes out as criticism. Your mother might say, "You should have gone to graduate school when you had the chance." Or ask you, "Don't you think you're wasting your time in that job?" Worse, she may compare you negatively with your sisters or friends.

Keep in mind that this is self-doubt at work! Although your mother has your best interests at heart, she may be caught up in concern and fear for your well-being and happiness. Because we live in a society that makes mothers responsible for how things turn out, she may feel she has to justify her position as a caring and concerned parent. How can you respond in these instances? By remaining connected to your own competence and not giving in to insecurity, you might simply acknowledge your mother's fears. Tell her, "I know you worry about me. Sometimes I do too." Then:

- Give your mother the details about how you overcame self-doubt in a specific work situation.

- Initiate a discussion on how the expectation to Have a Career is relatively recent for women. Ask her about how the work situation was for her when she was in her twenties, and how it is similar to or different from what your work and career options are now.

- Help your mother see that you are making the distinction between the pressure to Have a Career and deciding what you really want to do.

- Let your mother see your excitement about the job choices you are making so she can understand the passion you feel about work.

- Acknowledge her when she shows you support in a way that is positive for you.

- Plan together what to tell other relatives what you are doing about pursuing a career and why you are working at a particular job.

Tell your mother how much you appreciate it when she has helped you focus on your interests in the past and encouraged your talents. She will be pleased to hear the part she played, and as a result, will be even more affirming of your choices. Then, you and she will truly be "allies against self-doubt."

Helping your women friends. Sometimes friends have trouble with us when we are having trouble. They don't want to be dragged down by any insecurity either, especially if we're not good company or much fun to be with. So, once you've had some success against self-doubt, enlist your friends in supporting your efforts. As with your mother, fill them in on specific details of how you are overcoming self-doubt.

- Tell them when they are especially helpful in their advice about your work situation.

- Discuss the different ways they think "women's knowledge" is useful in the workplace.

- Notice how you can make a distinction between the "job" and the return of self-confidence, and celebrate the good career decisions that follow.

- Make yourself available to your friends to share your successful experiences, without imposing your ideas on them.

- Create rituals and plan celebrations to give each other mutual encouragement and support.

You may discover, unfortunately, that not everyone can be supportive in your success against self-doubt. Some of your friends may feel threatened and jealous when you achieve success or recognition in your career. Maybe you've even felt this way. So though your friends may not intend to do so, their criticism can be hurtful.

How can you handle this? Let's say you get a well-deserved promotion at work. You may hear, "You've really changed since you've been made assistant vice president at the bank." Or a friend might comment, "I think your performing at a comedy club is a waste of your talents." A version of self-doubt is making these friends compare themselves negatively to you, and so they unexpectedly attack instead of support you. They themselves may be struggling with insecurity, which could lead to jealousy over your success. This then keeps them from seeing your success is really that of overcoming self-doubt.

There's no good or easy way to address your friends' frustration, so it's often best simply to acknowledge what they are feeling. You might answer, "I know I've changed, but it's for the better because I feel more confident about myself." You could also say, "I'm sorry you think I'm wasting my talents, but I'm really happy with what I'm doing."

Remember, not everyone can be your ally, so choose your support system carefully. You want people who believe in you and are by your side as you leave fear and worry behind.

Helping the men in your life. Your father, brother, husband, boyfriend, or other male friends want to help in your quest for a career. While they probably have many useful hints and suggestions to offer about your career because the world of work is still in their domain, remember they may not think about things in the same way you do. Instead of asking them what they would do, try the following:

- Ask them to suggest an approach that your male boss or coworker might accept or listen to.

- Seek out specific advice about a particular topic at your job. Make sure you want to hear what they have to say.

- Tell them how much you want their acknowledgment and support. Explain exactly what you mean, so they will know how to give it, and that sometimes all you may want is a comforting hug.

- Be clear that you want them to hear your ideas and be open to your line of reasoning too.

The men in your life will be glad that you came to them for help and that you count them as your allies.

Don't forget that important people from your past can also be allies against self-doubt. Elaine's recollection of her grandmother's unconditional pride in her accomplishments inspires her to take action about her career. Think of friends and relatives who recognized your special gifts and talents, and what they might say to you now. Maybe your father used to tell you how he always loved to hear you sing and remind you that anything to do with the performing arts brought passion to your life. Or your best friend from high school who always admired your patience with the slower students in your class would encourage your decision to leave the business world and become a special education teacher.

Make a list of the specific times in the past when you were proud of what you were doing, and recall the persons who would have noticed your accomplishments at the time. Then, ask yourself who among them would not be surprised at how you are now successfully challenging the expectation to Have a Career. Think about what they might observe about you now that is a sign of your acting with confidence as you make decisions about your work life.

GOING FORWARD WITH COMPETENCE

Although your career is an important aspect of your identity, your success over self-doubt is the only true success. By facing

down this expectation, you have taken an important step to begin to pursue whatever job you desire, find meaning and passion
in your life through the work you choose, and define your life in
your own terms.

CHAPTER THREE

Make It on Your Own

COLLEEN, A RECENT graduate from the University of Washington, feels fortunate to have a good job in software development. "But it's a bottom-of-the-ladder position, the pay is low, and I'm afraid all the time," she says. "I thought once I finished school that I would be able to make enough money to support myself. Now it seems as if I'm getting more and more in debt."

As a young woman today, you are realistic about the fact that you must have the education and skills, as well as the financial know-how, to look after your own needs. Yet, as Colleen is discovering, the pressure to "Make It on Your Own" can be intimidating—especially when you consider the sheer enormity of your monthly bills and expenses. *Wanting* to be financially independent has been transformed into *having* to be financially independent, a frightening and often overwhelming responsibility that you now must face.

The expectation to Make It on Your Own begins even before college, and continues on through finding a career, getting married, and having children. It is a pressure that never lets up. As you start out on your own, keep in mind that the combination of the pressure to make it on your own and the need to have money to do so can be confusing and get you to lose sight of what you also truly want for yourself.

THE DILEMMA

The necessity for financial independence is a reality for women today. The world has changed, and you are no longer expected to depend exclusively on your husband for your economic needs. Although you'll probably eventually marry and have children, this will more likely happen in your late twenties or early thirties, so there may be a number of years when you will have to support yourself. After marriage, you will probably continue to work and contribute to your family's income. Most women worry about their finances and economic stability. According to a 1998 survey of 1,000 mothers and teenage daughters conducted by Yankelovich Partners, the number one concern of daughters and the number three concern of mothers is that they will not have enough money at some point in their lives. Yet, many young women have no particular template for how to handle financial concerns. Television commercials and peer pressure may teach you how to be a consumer but not how to make money work for you.

Unfortunately, most of us are not very good at talking about the specifics of money. Parents tell their children to be financially responsible but usually provide no details about how this is supposed to happen. If a family has a budget, it's not necessarily shared or discussed openly. When there are financial problems, parents will tell their children, "We don't have the money," or "You can't do that," without explaining the reasons why.

In a recent Girls Inc./Oppenheimer poll, three-quarters of adult women say they wish they knew more about money and how to use it wisely and effectively. It is no surprise, therefore, that most young women are stressed out by the pressure to Make It on Your Own. One positive response has been the growing number of financial literacy programs that are now available for girls as young as six years old. In high schools, colleges, and after-school programs throughout the country, girls and young women are being taught personal financial skills including learning how to save, invest, spend, budget, and prepare for future careers.

Each of us has our own unique combination of family background, values, beliefs, desires, and goals regarding issues concerning money. As a result, you are most likely struggling with some form of self-doubt from the pressure of the demand that you "should" be making it on your own. This insecurity interferes with your financial goals and preferences as well as your very real need to make a living. As you follow the stories of Colleen, Maria, and Jenny, notice how each woman works to overcome self-doubt as she deals with a different version of the expectation to Make It on Your Own.

Colleen's decision to be self-sufficient is based on the reality of having no one else to depend on for support. She struggles with paying her bills and making ends meet, and soon begins to doubt her own competence. Maria, on the other hand, is pleased to be financially independent. Yet, lately, she is feeling pressure from her family and friends to get married and have children, getting her to question the direction she has chosen for herself. Jenny, who you met as she struggled with the expectation to be with someone, chafes at the fact that her parents continue to support her. She is embarrassed and upset that she is not Making It on Her Own and loses confidence in herself and her own talents and skills.

NEEDING TO BE SELF-SUFFICIENT

After graduating from college with a major in computer software technology, Colleen, twenty-two, goes to work at a midsized computer company in the Seattle area. Although the job is pretty low level and doesn't pay much, at least it's work, and in product development, the area Colleen wants. Her parents have made sacrifices over the years to help pay for her education, so Colleen is relieved that she is finally in a position to support herself.

All through college Colleen struggled financially, even living at home for the first two years so she could save some money. Her independence is important to her, however, so with a part-time job and college loans Colleen is able to move out in her junior year. She still continues to live in the same apartment with her roommate, Karissa, splitting the expenses fifty-fifty.

Colleen feels certain she can make it on her own now that she's employed full time, although she is constantly worried about making ends meet. "I'd like to afford to buy nice clothes for work and decent furniture for my home," she says. "And I'd love to be able to entertain and have people over for dinner."

Colleen is overwhelmed by the sheer quantity of her bills, starting with her monthly expenses of rent, utilities, phone, and gas for her car. She can't afford cable television, and although she would like to have a cat, she's afraid of possible veterinarian bills. Colleen tries to buy food in bulk, but that requires an initial outlay of money. So she shops for bargains and clips coupons like her mother. Fortunately her car is paid for, but soon may require more repairs than she can afford. She also has to include a payment toward her college loan in her monthly budget. As a result, Colleen charges more to her credit card than she would like, including all of her entertainment. Her last bill was so high, however, that now she thinks twice about going out, which makes her feel more lonely and deprived.

It helps that there's a gym at work so Colleen can get some exercise and spend time with her colleagues from the office. She also eats in the company cafeteria where the food is inexpensive and there's always someone to talk with. But Colleen still has to think twice before accepting invitations from her friends to go clubbing and dancing on weekends. If she says yes, she worries that she's spending money she doesn't have; if she declines, she worries that her friends won't ask her to join them again.

Colleen's roommate, Karissa, doesn't seem to have the same money concerns, however, and recently ordered cable television for the apartment. Colleen is grateful, even though they both know that she can't afford to pay her half. "It's embarrassing to have to admit that I can't pull my share of the load," she says. "Karissa doesn't put any pressure on me, so it's really my issue. Still, I wish this weren't so hard and I didn't feel so alone about my situation."

Although Colleen wants to be financially independent, she really has no choice: There's no one else to turn to for support. The pressure from the expectation to Make It on Your Own is making her life difficult, and she is scared to death she won't be able to make ends meet.

When I ask Colleen what she would call the problem, she quickly says, "Fear. I'm afraid all the time. I'm so upset that sometimes I can't even eat. Now it's affecting my sleep. I have a hard time falling asleep, then wake up several times during the night. I'm exhausted when I have to get up in the morning."

I tell her that I know the fear is real. I then ask her what she thinks has happened to the confidence she used to have that she could meet this challenge.

Colleen thinks about my question. "I guess the fear is so all consuming that it's taken away my confidence," she says. "I assumed that once I finished school I would be able to make enough money to support myself. But now I feel as if I'm getting deeper and deeper in debt."

I point out that making enough money to support yourself and knowing how to manage your finances are important issues. "I imagine you have the know-how and the skills to do that," I say. "Do you think the fear may be blinding you to your own sense of competence?"

"I'm sure that's true," Colleen readily admits. "This is a struggle. But I've never been one to give up on myself, and I've always prided myself on being resilient. If nothing else, my parents taught me I could do anything I wanted."

I ask Colleen to consider how the fear surrounding this expectation got so big.

"Somewhere along the line my wanting to be financially independent became both a need and a should," she replies. "The pressure to support myself was overwhelming, and once that happened, the fear just slipped in. Now it feels as if the fear has taken over my life. It gets me to obsess about my monthly bills, it's constantly on my mind when I think about doing something for fun, it's even affecting my eating and sleeping."

Colleen explains that she's beginning to realize how little she knows about money. "I suppose I could learn," she says. "My parents didn't teach me about managing my finances, even though they seem to be good at it. I'm also impatient that I'm not earning as much as I would like. I keep telling myself that I have a good job in a field that's wide open for advancement. Not only that, I'm a quick study, so I'll probably get promoted sooner rather than later. I just have to make do for now and continue to believe in myself."

I suggest to Colleen that fear and self-doubt may make that difficult to do.

"Exactly," Colleen responds. "Once I overcome the self-doubt, then it's straight ahead, no holds barred. I know I can do it."

Colleen notices how much fear is in her life and how it controls her thinking and desires. As she understands that the fear is coming from the persistent pressure of the expectation to Make It on Your Own, she begins to trust herself to get past it. Colleen is well aware she has to support herself, but she also realizes that becoming financially independent is what she wants for herself.

As a start, Colleen checks out some Web sites on money management and financial planning. Using this practical advice, she draws up a budget that includes a little money for entertainment. She begins to make distinctions between what she would like to spend her money on and what items can wait for later. Colleen also comes clean with her friends, explaining how her limited funds sometimes make it difficult for her to join them on the weekends. "I don't have the money right now," she tells them, "but check with me next time."

Colleen now realizes she can be very competent in the area of financial independence. Although she has known this all along, the fear had masked her understanding. By overcoming fear, she remembers the times when she was confident about her handling of money matters.

CONFLICTING DESIRES

Maria is a graduate of the University of Texas at San Antonio with a degree in environmental studies. Now, at twenty-four, she has a steady job with a geological survey firm doing environmental impact reports. Maria loves her work and was recently promoted to a position with greater responsibility.

Maria lives at home where she has been taking care of her mother since her father died four years ago. Her mother is very proud of her accomplishments, as is Maria's fiancé, Alfredo. But something is wrong. Maria is constantly getting pressure from her brothers and sisters to settle down, and Alfredo is now talking about their setting a wedding date. Even her mother is hinting to Maria about her stopping work and thinking about having babies.

In some ways Maria is not surprised. She also wants to get married and have a family. But she doesn't want to give up her career like some of her friends have after they got married. Elena, who is Maria's closest friend in the world, can't understand her dilemma. "I would love to find someone like Alfredo who wants to take care of me," Elena tells her. "Who needs the hassle of worrying all the time how you're going to make ends meet? I, personally, would welcome the chance to be at home with my kids and not have to go to the office every day."

Although Maria is proud about how she has shaped her own life, doubts are beginning to creep in. "Maybe I should get married and start a family," she thinks. "I can always go back to work later. Why is it so important to me to be able to take care of myself financially? I've shown I can do it—I even support my mother. Maybe it's time to let Alfredo take care of me."

The doubts take the form of constant questioning, and Maria can't stop wondering if she's really as happy as she imagines. She notices that most of her friends from high school are married, many already with toddlers. Is she being too independent for her own good? Gradually, Maria becomes more and more anxious that she may be on the wrong track.

I ask Maria to put a name to the problem that is getting her to question herself and the choices she has made.

"I would call it 'second-guessing,' " Maria says. "There's so much pressure from all sides to stop working and be a wife and mother. Alfredo doesn't come out and say anything but I think he would like us to get married sooner rather than later. Eventually I want that too, but it's always been important for me to pursue my work and be financially independent. Now I just don't know."

Maria explains that she makes more money than Alfredo, who is a high school science teacher, and that two incomes will be good for their future family. "Why would I want to give up my earning power, not to mention a job I love?" she asks. "Before I was on my own, I thought a CD was something that went into my car sound system. Now I have savings in a CD account as well as a retirement fund. I've made it a point to educate myself financially."

I ask Maria to think about how "second-guessing" is affecting her.

"It's making me think I shouldn't want to be financially independent, that I should be content to depend on Alfredo," she replies. "It's making me question if I've been right to pursue my own way. I'm beginning to wonder if something is wrong with me. My future used to seem so clear, but now I'm not even sure what my priorities are."

Maria decides to speak with Dr. Sally Gonzales, her former teacher and advisor at the university. Sally is chair of the environmental studies program and the mother of three young children. She is also Mexican American and familiar with many of the cultural issues that Maria is currently facing. Maria is not only excited to bring her mentor up to date on what she's been doing since she left school but also wants to ask Sally how she deals with any conflicting desires she may have about her career and family.

As Maria tells Sally about her job and her engagement to Alfredo, she realizes once again how important it is for her to be financially independent. Her renewed energy makes her answer to Sally's question about what she really wants easier than she had thought.

"I want to be able to work and have a family, like you do," Maria says. "It's very important to me to continue to earn my own money after Alfredo and I get married. I would like to contribute to our family's finances as well as keep on supporting my mother. I also want to share responsibilities with Alfredo rather than depend on him for everything."

Sally considers Maria's dilemma. "Then share your desire with him too," she advises Maria. "Alfredo loves and respects you. He may even be relieved when he hears that you're not expecting him to be the sole provider in the family. Maybe that responsibility feels like a burden to him."

Maria realizes she can still want to get married and feel supported by Alfredo, both financially and emotionally, as well as make it on her own. It's possible for Alfredo and her to share their lives together, including children, home, work—and financial matters.

Maria comes to understand that the problem is not that she is making money or that she can't depend on Alfredo; the problem is the second-guessing that gets her to doubt herself and question her own desires. Maria wants to be independent and knows she is competent enough to make it on her own. She also wants to marry Alfredo and contribute her fair share as his partner. She's proud of her decision.

FINANCIAL FREEDOM

Jenny's kayaking trip to New Zealand is every bit the adventure she had hoped for. She returns home to Minneapolis to decompress before she gets ready to look for a job. Jenny's parents have told her to take all the time she needs to find work that is important to her. She's fortunate, as she knows that her parents are affluent enough to support her as she starts out. Yet, Jenny finds herself beginning to feel pressure to find meaningful work so she won't have to depend on them any more.

Jenny didn't know anything about money matters when she was growing up. She was aware that her parents seemed to have enough money to do as they wished, and she rarely was turned down for anything she wanted. As Jenny got older, especially in college where she saw some of her friends scrimping and saving, she realized how lucky she was. She was somewhat embarrassed by the fact that she didn't need to worry about her expenses and bills, however, and soon came to understand that financial freedom is not necessarily the same as financial independence.

Now, after college and the kayaking trip, Jenny decides that her heart is back in Madison, where she got her degree in political science at the University of Wisconsin. She also thinks it may be easier to find a job there; she has kept up with some of the staff members in the mayor's office where she interned during her senior year. She hopes that she will begin to experience the financial independence she really wants now that she can be on her own and pay her own bills.

Soon, however, Jenny finds that self-sufficiency is much more difficult than she had imagined. She needs to turn to her parents for her first and last month's rent on her new apartment, they're paying her car and medical insurance, and until she finds work, they're also taking care of her car payments and gasoline bills. Jenny is somewhat bothered that she has to accept support from her parents, but they seem fine about giving it to her. Also, they never attach any strings to their help, at least as far as she can see. Jenny knows she should be grateful to have her parents' money as a buffer and security to pursue what she wants in life. Even so, their financial support, which used to feel like a safety net, now seems more like an albatross around her neck.

Jenny's desire to make it on her own is beginning to feel more and more like a pressure. Depending on her parents' money makes her think she's inadequate and incompetent in her attempt to live independently. Sometimes she thinks about telling them that she doesn't need their support and can make ends meet on her own. But Jenny is still looking for a job she cares about and nothing seems to be out there. She wonders if she's being too picky, reluctant to work because it's not really a true necessity for her.

Doubts begin to creep in as Jenny questions herself, her desires, and her current state in life. She's aware that her upper-middle-class background affords her opportunities that some of her friends may not have. But the flip side of her family's affluence is that it is makes her question her ability to be self-sufficient. The doubts not only get her to feel bad about herself but also make her hide her true financial situation from her friends and downplay her own talents and skills.

In truth, Jenny is very competent. She graduated with honors, she continues to educate herself and reads constantly, and she is active in several community-based organizations in Madison. She has lost perspective, however, and wonders if she'll ever be able find a job to support her. The thought of having to depend on her parents indefinitely embarrasses her and makes her ashamed.

As the shame grows, Jenny becomes more and more stuck about the direction to take in her postcollege life. She knows she can't just hang out in Madison indefinitely. Jenny still believes she could have a huge impact on shaping public policy on the local level, but is so caught up in shame about her financial situation that she can't think clearly what to do next. The end result is that she does nothing.

"Talking about money is really hard for me," Jenny says. "We never spoke about it in my family and still don't. It feels like I have nowhere to turn."

I mention that many people don't seem to talk about money very well, even with close friends and family members. I suggest that it might be more helpful to talk about the shame and doubt first rather than the money.

"Naming the problem 'self-doubt' or 'shame' seems to help," Jenny tells me. "It's a lot like the 'fear' I experienced in my relationship with Lela. I feel paralyzed. I don't know what to do. I probably have more options than most of my friends, because I have more financial freedom than many people I know. It's shame that keeps me from moving forward."

I ask Jenny to notice how shame is affecting her on a daily basis, how it's keeping her stuck and making her feel bad about herself. Jenny recites the ways: She feels paralyzed, she can't seem to find a job that interests her, she's embarrassed about having to depend on her parents, and she can't think clearly.

As Jenny continues her list, she begins to realize that she has to do something to be free of shame and doubt and take charge of her life. She wants to educate herself on becoming financially independent and learning how to make it on her own. Jenny knows that there may be no one she can easily talk to about money issues, so she starts by enrolling in an evening class at the university specifically directed to help women understand and be in charge of their money. She also goes to her neighborhood bookstore and browses in the self-help section to see if she can find answers to some of her financial questions. (See "Resources," p. 231.)

Jenny is greatly relieved to see that she is not alone in her fears, that economic concerns are universal and widespread. This new knowledge and awareness helps her think about the role of money in her life, both now and in the future. She recognizes that her fortunate economic situation allows her to view money as a means to an end and not the ultimate goal. She also begins to understand that she doesn't have to apologize for her situation.

Jenny's realization frees her to see that she has the luxury of moving carefully to find a meaningful job. By gaining some perspective on her situation, Jenny sees that it's okay to be patient. She believes she will be financially self-sufficient one day and will no longer have to depend on her parents. This belief is exciting to Jenny, and her next days and weeks are spent more thoughtfully pursuing job possibilities that interest her.

Jenny also realizes that financial freedom is not making her free; paradoxically it is keeping her stuck. By challenging the expectation to Make It on Your Own, she can begin to relax about her temporary economic dependence on her parents. She can start off by working at a job she likes that may not pay that much but will lead to her eventual advancement. Jenny believes she will achieve financial independence and learns she can be more patient with her current situation as her life unfolds.

WHAT CAN YOU DO?

Make It on Your Own is an expectation that can begin to create twinges of doubt in your life even before you finish high school. It can push you to take jobs to make extra spending money, to pay for your college tuition, or support yourself as soon as you leave your parents' home. Our society increasingly sees women as needing and wanting to be financially independent. However, as you know, the desire to be on your own monetarily has the double whammy of being both an expectation and a need. When this loaded expectation is in place, it can pressure you to question your ability to be economically self-sufficient, lead to self-doubt, and keep you stuck and not knowing where to turn.

Let's say you decide to move home right after college in order to save on rent while you're looking for a good job. Now, you have to deal with the fact that your parents are still paying your bills. Or maybe you have a job, but it's at the bottom rung of the ladder in your field, or not in your field at all, and you know the salary won't pay the rent. You see friends and former classmates in high-paying jobs. You wonder if you should forget trying to Make It on Your Own and apply to graduate school. Your parents say, "We'll help you out." Or, "You can live here."

But they always add, "As long as you're going to school or working." Or, "This isn't open-ended. We want you to be able to support yourself by such-and-such a time." These words literally
feed the expectation to Make It on Your Own, resulting in more
self-doubt.

Gradually, it begins to dawn on you that you might have to
struggle for a lot longer than you thought. You become scared
you may not be able to control your debts, manage your spending habits, budget your money, or afford the necessities—and
luxuries—you want. You don't want to work at a job that's not
challenging, especially when you know you're well educated and
could be very good at whatever you put your mind to.

Think about how the expectation—and need—to Make It on
Your Own creates pressure for you and how it shows up in your
life. Although this expectation is a close cousin to the previous
expectation to Have a Career, it differs in one major respect: It
focuses on your need to know how to support yourself and be independent economically, to make money and learn how to use it
wisely and well. Of course you have to have a job to do so, but
now your questions about your career are inextricably entwined
with being self-sufficient.

By now, you know that the pressure of every expectation can
lead to self-doubt and sneak into the tiniest event or interaction in
your life. For example, doubt about your financial situation and
earning capabilities can show up when you're out with your
friends: You begin to compare how you spend money with how
they spend money—who has more ready cash, who pops for
drinks, who pays for parking, who fronts for concert tickets,
who never seems to have money for anything, and so on.

Self-doubt can also make an entrance when you sit down to
pay your monthly bills. You may find yourself asking if you should

CASH OR CREDIT?

Do you pay your monthly bills with your credit card?

- Phone
- Utilities
- Gym membership
- Internet access

What other expenses do you use your credit card for?

- Car gas and repairs
- Restaurants
- Groceries
- Entertainment

What bills do you actually pay from your checking account?

- Student loan
- Monthly rent
- Car payment and insurance
- Medical insurance
- Entertainment

Do you have a budget?
Do you know how much you make and spend every month?
Do you save any money?

be budgeting your money better, saving more, or spending differently. You wonder if you're even financially literate. You certainly didn't learn much about the basics of personal finance from your parents and had no classes in school to help you—except maybe basic math where you learned how to balance your checkbook. You begin to distrust your skills in the area of money management and wonder if you will ever have financial security.

Pay attention to your everyday experience with the pressure of this expectation. Does it give you physical symptoms such as an upset stomach, tightness in your chest, a stiff neck, an aching back? Does it make you feel irritable, judgmental, agitated, nervous? Do you find yourself asking over and over: What am I doing with my life? Who cares about me? What good am I?

If the issue of money is becoming all consuming and you are experiencing some kind of distress connected with the need to be financially independent, then the expectation to Make It on Your Own is putting pressure on you and creating insecurity in your life.

RECOGNIZE AND NAME THE PROBLEM

As with the previous expectations, start by noticing specific ways you are being influenced by the pressure to Make It on Your Own. You may be constantly worried about your finances. Maybe you're not concerned but should be and are blithely spending every penny you have. You may be hypersensitive about your finances with your friends or your partner or work colleagues—not to mention your parents. You may not be telling a soul about your doubts. Perhaps you're filled with fear like Colleen, doubting your choices like Maria, or embarrassed and ashamed like Jenny.

Think about what you would call this problem: Is it "doubt," "discouragement," "fear," "worry," "second-guessing," "oversensitivity," or something else? Whatever you name it, remember that the problem is some form of self-doubt. Colleen recognizes it as "fear" that overwhelms and consumes her. Maria calls it a "second-guessing" and sees how it forces her to question her decisions. Jenny names it "shame," which keeps her paralyzed and stops her from going forward in her life. What will you name it?

Next, notice all the ways this problem affects you. How does it appear in your life? Do you experience the problem more often when you are with others or mostly when you're alone? Does it get you to compare and judge your financial situation by how others are doing? Or is the problem more likely to get you to obsess about the way you spend money? Your lack of money? Your need for money?

Consider some of the entry points for the different versions of self-doubt and how they confuse you about your current financial situation. Fear enters Colleen's life when she realizes that her job will provide only enough money to support her essential living expenses and none of the extras she would like. Although Maria wants to be financially independent, second-guessing gets her to question if making it on her own is what she really wants and if she should simply allow someone else to take care of her. Shame captures Jenny as she searches for a way to be financially independent through her own efforts, not continuing to be dependent on her parents and their money.

What is self-doubt doing to you?

- Is it keeping you stuck and paralyzed?

- Is it clouding your goals?

- Does it make you want to delay your career?

- Is it getting you to think about going back to school as your only option?

- Does it tell you to live at home and never leave?

- Does it keep you stuck in a nothing job?

- Is it getting you to bury your head in the sand and keep charging up that credit card?

- Is it telling you something good will happen through pure luck, like winning the lottery?

Your answers to these questions may help you decide that you would like self-doubt out of your life. By becoming free of its influence, you can begin to think clearly about how to Make It on Your Own—but on your terms.

Once you notice some of the negative effects of self-doubt, you will probably find it helpful to enlist help in getting clear of the problem. When Colleen realizes that fear is getting her to not believe in herself, she decides she might need some guidance about managing money as well as be clear with her friends on what she can afford. When Maria understands that second-guessing is getting her to question her desire to Make It on Her Own, she goes to her former professor and mentor for direction and validation. Jenny understands that shame is keeping her stuck, and finds books and classes that inspire and guide her.

Self-doubt is isolating; it confines us like prisoners in solitary confinement. It gets us to think we are "in this alone" and have to "do it by ourselves." By asking others to join you in recognizing self-doubt, you are using an anti-isolation tactic, which is a potent weapon for keeping that doubt at bay.

As we have seen before, as self-doubt—or whatever the problem is for you—becomes less powerful, you will be able to notice more clearly how it arises from the pressure of the expectation and need to Make It on Your Own. In addition, by sharing your thoughts with others, it is usually easier to see the expectation for what it is: a powerful "should" that is getting you to go on automatic or blinding you to your own desires. You can then more easily face this very real need to become economically self-sufficient. By doing so you are already taking the next step.

UNDERSTAND AND CHALLENGE THE EXPECTATION

As women enter the different professions of the work force in greater numbers and become financial players as well as influential consumers, our relationship to the world of money changes dramatically. We are now expected to be—and need to be—financially independent.

When you leave the safety of home and college, you are supposed to make it on your own. The time is past when you could count on being taken care of; perhaps it was never really there, but the idea that your husband would provide was the dominant belief. Now you have to take care of yourself. And you most likely want to.

Make It on Your Own is not only an expectation but also a very real necessity. The powerful combination of the need as well as the demand to be financially self-sufficient can be confusing and create intense pressure. As you begin to challenge this expectation within the realistic context of your financial situation, you will be better able to understand why you are experiencing such distress. Then you can separate out what you really want both from what you think is expected of you and from what you have to do to Make It on Your Own.

Achieving financial independence is not easy nor does it

happen instantly. You may have to develop patience, knowing you might need to work up the ladder. You must also keep in perspective the reality that in many cases women still are not paid as much as men for equal work.

Your responses to the following statements can help you make important distinctions about what is influencing you in your quest to Make It on Your Own, and is a good starting point for examining how you view your economic present and future.

1. Being financially independent means

   - being on my own,
   - creating my own life,
   - no longer being dependent on my parents.

2. Wanting to maintain a certain standard of living is probably connected to the lifestyle I had when I was growing up.

3. There are certain skills about managing money that I need to learn, including budgeting, saving, and investing.

4. I most likely will need to wait patiently to develop the kind of job I want and make the income I would like.

Challenging the expectation to Make It on Your Own is a battle with many fronts. It's important to start by defining what front you are facing.

Colleen knows she can make it on her own and that she wants to. She also knows she has to because she has no one else to depend on. When Colleen separates her desire and her belief in herself from the fear that comes from the pressure to be self-sufficient, she understands why this expectation feels so demanding.

Once Maria faces the second-guessing, she can make the distinction between two things she wants: to Make It on Her Own and to have a family. She realizes one doesn't have to cancel out the other, and her mutual desires can coexist.

Jenny manages to overcome the shame that has blinded her. She can then see that she is in the unique position to have both financial freedom and financial independence.

What realizations come to you as you expose self-doubt as a pressure from the expectation to Make It on Your Own? List some of the many fronts that you are challenging:

- Do you want to be financially independent knowing that you have no one else to depend on, but also knowing you have the necessary skills to make it on your own?

- Do you have seemingly competing desires, wanting to be economically self-sufficient, but also wanting to be married and have children?

- Do you know that you can count on your parents for some things, but that eventually you can create your own independence separate from them?

As you consider these questions, see what thoughts pop into your head. Maybe you're remembering times and places when you were clear about your financial goals or what you were doing to achieve them. Perhaps you recall periods in your life when the expectation to Make It on Your Own had less power over you, and you were better able to describe your preferences. These events and incidents are important memories. They are also entry points into our next step where you will connect to your own intuition and to your past experiences of confidence and competence in the area of economic self-sufficiency.

CONNECT TO WHAT YOU VALUE AND BELIEVE

As you reflect on past events where you were clear about your financial goals and acted in ways that were consistent with them, you will undoubtedly begin to connect with your own values about money and success. Even though financial security is important to you, how you think about making and spending money will determine the decisions you make to attain your goals. What amounts of money do you want/need to live well? What does "living well" mean to you? What is your attachment to material things? How does your relationship to possessions influence your decisions about financial security and money management? Regardless of your personal values, how do you distinguish between what you want and what society expects of you?

Colleen, Maria, and Jenny each have different values about having and using money. As you answer the following questions, think about how your values influence your version of what it means to be financially independent.

Recall past experiences or events when you acted in accord with your own values and goals.

• Are you filled with fear that you won't be able to support yourself or can you connect with confidence to your abilities and achievements?

• What do you know about managing money in a way that allows you to meet your financial obligations?

• Do you accept financial support if you need it realizing this does not necessarily compromise your independence and autonomy?

• Do you have the perspective to see that having and making money can sometimes take time?

• Can you be gracious with others who don't seem to have to worry about money?

• If you do have money and financial stability, do you notice your good fortune and show generosity with what you have?

Sometimes it's helpful to talk to your parents and ask them what they think about money and how they managed it when you were growing up. If your parents seem to avoid speaking about financial issues, you may find taking this step of opening a conversation with them a bit awkward. It may help to come at it sideways; for example, ask them how they passed their financial skills and values on to you. Then you can reconnect with what you do know with confidence and search for information to increase your knowledge in the areas where you need to learn more.

It may also be helpful to recall memories or bits and pieces of conversations in your life that were related to money. Maybe your mother once told you, "I want to support your career choice, but I don't want you to make a decision based solely on how much money you will earn." Or your father said, "Always act like you have a million dollars." You might ask them what they meant by their words. What values did they want you to incorporate? You could also imagine what advice they would give you now as you connect with what your values are about money and what you know about how to reach financial stability.

What is your level of financial literacy?

- How did you learn about money skills such as budgeting, spending, investing, and saving?

- What skills do you currently practice in your use of money?

- How do you go about learning new skills? Where would you go to learn how to use money wisely?

If your parents were not so adept at communicating to you about how to master your personal finances, you may think you have little in the way of specific skills from your past to recall. However, as you conquer self-doubt, it is likely that possibilities will open up for you to begin to notice what you need to do to become secure in your pursuit of financial independence.

The key is for you to reconnect not only with your own values about money but also with your knowledge about how to earn, spend, budget, and invest. The reality is that all of us need to survive, pay our bills, and support ourselves. Think about what you know about being self-sufficient, managing your own lifestyle, and using money well. Do you think you make financial choices wisely? How did you learn to do so? What pleases you about the money decisions you make?

Because the pressure to be financially independent is especially strong for women in their twenties, self-doubt is constantly around. It is important to recognize this feeling and continue to challenge the expectation so that you can reconnect to your personal competence about financial matters. It will also help to share your answers, impressions, and experiences with your friends and others who support you as you face the pressure of the mandate to Make It on Your Own.

SEEK ALLIES AGAINST SELF-DOUBT

As you go through the process of separating from self-doubt and challenging the expectation to Make It on Your Own, the search for allies can be especially difficult in three important ways. First, the obligation to be financially independent and Make It on Your Own may seem to cancel out the option that you can ask for help. Even though women traditionally thrive in relationships and seek out connections with others, this expectation seems to require us to do it ourselves.

The second difficulty is that this expectation is wrapped around issues of money, possessions, and material items. As a result, it is imperative that you be as clear as possible regarding your values and philosophy about money. Seeking allies means finding others who either share your way of thinking or appreciate your beliefs. It also may mean that they know something about what your struggle for financial independence really is.

Third, talking about money is just not part of our culture. Breaking this taboo can be very hard and in certain circumstances impossible. It is imperative to remember that what you are experiencing is less about issues concerning money and more about how self-doubt gets in the way of your discovering and doing what works for you.

The process of seeking out allies begins with the first step of recognizing and naming the problem and continues through the process of overcoming self-doubt, challenging the expectation to Make It on Your Own, and continuing the connection to your own knowledge and competence in financial matters. Speaking openly about money will probably always be somewhat difficult, but as you overcome the fear and worry, you will find that you will learn how to talk about money issues and then be better prepared to clearly address your financial needs.

The following questions will help you focus your thoughts about how and what to talk about with your potential allies.

- What attributes would you like your allies to possess?

- What knowledge about how to be self-sufficient do you have that you would want them to appreciate?

- Who in the past would know about that knowledge?

- What would they say about you now?

- Who knows about your values surrounding money?

- Who both in the past and present would most appreciate how you are performing your life in a way that is consistent with your knowledge and values?

Although you need allies and don't want to feel isolated and alone, the truth is that no one else holds your personal values and knowledge in exactly the way you do. Everyone's relationship to money and financial security is uniquely their own. Sometimes you just have to trust your own intuition and believe in yourself, even if others give you contrary advice. Therefore, stay firm in paying attention to what you know and trusting what you believe in. Follow your heart, and then ask others to be your allies—to believe in you and respect your vision.

Who might you go to first to enlist as an ally? You may

wonder if your mother understands the pressure you experience to Make It on Your Own. Here's how you can help her to help you.

Helping your mother. Chances are your mother worked when you were growing up, although your father was most likely the primary breadwinner in the family. If you ask your mother if she expected to be financially independent when she was your age, she would probably say, "No, not really. I assumed that I would work but that my income would be used to supplement what my husband provided."

You might have to help your mother see what it's like for you now. Let her know that you envision yourself as the one responsible for your life. Tell her that doesn't mean you don't want a partner; in fact, you probably do want to get married and have children someday and work together with your husband to make financial decisions.

- Remind your mother that society has different expectations for women today than when she was growing up, and you know her experience was different from yours.

- Let her know how self-doubt comes up about your problems with money and what you have done to overcome it.

- Tell her you appreciate her part in teaching you the tools you need to be successful in the financial realm.

- Be specific about what you learned from her about managing money, budgeting, and spending wisely.

- Let her know you are grateful for all that she taught you, not only about money matters but also about how to stay confident in the face of doubt.

Your conversations will depend on your mother's experience and your relationship with her, so think carefully about how she can understand and support your successes.

There may be other women, older than you, who serve as mentors in your life. Like Maria, you may have a teacher from high school or college who understands and appreciates your values. Perhaps you have an aunt or godmother with whom you have always been able to talk. Having such women in your life can be a wonderful gift, as they bring a longer view to the problem than women of your peer group can offer. In addition, they most likely won't have the same worries and fears that your mother may carry for you.

Asking a mentor to be a member of your ally group is fairly straightforward. It requires simply that you describe your struggles and let her know your goals. And often, she will ask you questions to help you clarify what it is you want, what you have found helpful, and how you can continue to live consistently with your values. Self-doubt is an equal opportunity employer, however, and it can also boss around your mentor. It may get her to give you unwanted advice, tell you endlessly about her experiences, or caution you unnecessarily.

As with others you invite to join your group of allies, think carefully about what your mentor needs to know so she can be helpful to you. Although your message may not always produce the desired results with your mother and your mentors, keep trying. They really do want to help and appreciate it when you show them how.

Helping your women friends. Like you, your peers are probably being pressured by the same expectation to Make It on Your Own. You may be able to share experiences together and provide mutual acknowledgement and appreciation. You will need to be vigilant with your friends, though, to keep self-doubt from sneaking up on you.

- Remind them of your intention to stay anchored in your commitment to pursue your financial goals.

- Develop ways to help each other notice when self-doubt makes an appearance and you have success over it.

- Let your allies know when they do or say something especially helpful.

- Be clear with your friends about what you can and cannot afford to spend, and ask them to do that for you too.

- Plan a get-together where you each specifically share what you've learned about money management. Pool your ideas and compare notes about what you know.

You may find that your friends are uneasy talking about money; some may not want you to know that they also have trouble with their bills and debts. Others may decide that their economic situation is none of your business. Remember, the problem isn't about money matters; it's self-doubt about our competence in creating financial independence in a way that fits us. Remind your friends who the enemy really is, and celebrate your mutual victories in overcoming self-doubt around this expectation.

Helping the men in your life. You may be fortunate and be able to easily go to your father for support and advice. He may feel confident in the realm of financial independence, as his training in the area has been lifelong and intense. Your father may also understand, better than some women, the pressure you feel to be responsible for your own financial situation. Although he may try immediately to fix your situation instead of listening to how self-doubt has entered your life and offering support, it's important to listen to what he has to say. As always, be clear about what you really want from him—not his solutions as much as his caring.

What about your boyfriend, husband, brother, and other male friends? Your boyfriend or husband may not want to hear about your financial woes because he may be facing expectations too—one of which is that he should be taking care of you. This may lead to his feeling ashamed. On the other hand, if you tell him about your money struggles, it may bring up his own worries, which might get him to be overly concerned about your dilemma, and he may feel inadequate about the pursuit of his own goals.

Although the man in your life probably prefers that you don't have to depend solely on him financially, he most likely thinks that he should be the main source of financial support in the family. Remember Sally's advice to Maria and invite your husband or boyfriend to work with you to create a plan for financial interdependence that both of you find acceptable. By combining your joint expertise and experience, you can start defining your life as a couple and design a unique template for facing self-doubt and challenging this expectation as a team.

Your brothers and other male friends, relatives, and teachers may have important ideas for you too. However, don't lose sight of the fact that the answer to your problem is not simply to fix your money problems: It is to keep self-doubt at bay. Let the men in your life know how much their encouragement means to you; tell them what you find helpful and not so helpful. Most important, tell them you need their support.

GOING FORWARD WITH COMPETENCE

By now you are clear that the culprit is self-doubt. The very real difficulties in knowing how to make, spend, and save money can make you anxious and insecure. Because you want to be financially independent, however, you can challenge the expectation and remember that you can learn how to manage money matters and take care of your financial life with confidence.

CHAPTER FOUR

Look Good, Be Thin

NATALIE, TWENTY-FIVE, IS the assistant fashion editor of a teen magazine in New York City. She loves her work, and living in Manhattan is both exciting and glamorous. Since she took the job six months ago, however, Natalie is finding herself becoming more and more preoccupied with how she looks and what she weighs. She is concerned about how self-conscious she's feeling about her appearance.

"I've always been very secure about my sense of style, not to mention my figure," Natalie says. "Now all I do is compare myself to the other editors at the magazine, even the models we use in our fashion spreads. No matter what I do, it seems as if I can't measure up to everyone else. Even though I know I'm judging myself against really high standards, it bothers me that

I don't think I'm as thin and put together as the other women are."

Because we relate to the world around us through our bodies, our identities are tied to our physical appearance. In addition, there are accepted standards and specifications in society for a woman's physical beauty based on her weight, body shape and size, fitness, and so on. The result is that the expectation "Look Good, Be Thin," more than any other, speaks to women of who they are. Society's standards of beauty wedge their way into your thinking, and become your standards without you even realizing it. The power of this expectation transforms into a mandate with potentially damaging effects, both psychological and physical. At its most extreme, this expectation can lead to eating problems, which can have devastating consequences.

Although women of all ages are concerned about their body image, Look Good, Be Thin exerts great pressure on women in their twenties and thirties. You are constantly being bombarded by messages to improve and change your appearance, your body size and shape, your diet, your workout plan, your choice of clothes, and your overall strategy to enhance your looks. If you find that you fall short of society's ideal standards for beauty and thinness—which most of us do—you feel insecure, uncertain, and bad about yourself. You may even withdraw and pull within, your fears too great to speak out loud.

Look Good, Be Thin tells you that no matter how competent you are in other areas of your life, your happiness and success are determined by your physical appearance. The problem, however, is *not* about diet or fitness or fashion: It is about self-doubt. As we zero in on the insecurity that this expectation creates, you will see how it takes you away from a relationship of integrity with your own body. You will then learn ways to overcome its power so you can connect to yourself with confidence.

THE DILEMMA

"Look at these models," says a young woman staring at a bathing suit magazine in a Garry Trudeau *Doonesbury* comic strip. "Wouldn't it be cool to be that gorgeous?" Her friend replies, "Well, yes, but you have to remember that their body type is not actually found in nature. Becoming the new feminine ideal requires just the right combination of insecurity, bulimia, and surgery!"

A negative body image greatly affects our feelings of esteem and self-worth. The pressure to Look Good, Be Thin is relentless, and keeping up includes such basic maintenance as exercise, diet, facials, manicures, hair coloring, and shopping for the latest fashions, to name a few. In addition, the options available to maintain a body type "not actually found in nature" have drastically increased. Many women, as a matter of course, undergo tummy tucks, liposuction, and breast enhancement; Botox and other spin-offs are no longer just for middle-aged women.

Most of us assume that body shape and eating habits are more or less within our control. Yet, the pressure to meet specific acceptable and desirable ideals of beauty—even if they're based on unrealistic criteria or airbrushed media portrayals—can create enormous anxiety and self-doubt. We judge our appearance against the enviable images of our favorite movie stars or fashionable celebrities. We compare ourselves to women at the gym, the shopping center, a favorite drinking spot, the company cafeteria.

Whether we feel less than others or look better than some, evaluation sets us up and leaves us ripe for the emergence of self-doubt.

The expectation to Look Good, Be Thin is extremely isolating. Even though we may share our concerns and worries about our weight or appearance with friends, we rarely address the core issue: our fears, our shame, our obsessions, our self-doubt. Secrecy increases our isolation, leaving us unable to have an honest dialogue with even those who are closest to us. We talk in code ("I guess I'm going to have to spend more time at the gym."); we fish for compliments ("Do you think I look fat in this outfit?"); we flatter our friends ("I swear I can't tell that you gained three pounds."). The bottom line? No one believes anyone, and we all question the sincerity of others.

Comparison and isolation intensify the power of self-doubt and conspire to keep us from acting and speaking openly about our fears. For example, instead of admitting that you're nervous about gaining weight when you're out having lunch with your friends, you may pretend not to be hungry and order a small salad, which you barely touch. Or, if you're trying on a form-fitting T-shirt and are pinching and poking to make sure no little fat rolls show, you will not let yourself believe the salesperson who tells you the top is just right for you. Or, when your boyfriend looks at you in a certain way, you become convinced that he thinks you're fat or not sexy enough even though he may deny it over and over.

There is no winning when the expectation to Look Good, Be Thin takes over your life. The irresistible urge to compare makes you constantly wonder if you measure up to the standards of beauty so prized by our society—until you're positive that you don't. Isolation keeps you locked in self-doubt that is so powerful that you can't talk about how you're feeling. Making distinctions regarding why you do what you do becomes almost impossible, not to mention the different cultural and ethnic values related to body image and appearance. No wonder you're confused and overwhelmed; it's difficult to know what you really believe or feel.

The struggle against the pervasive influence of this expectation in your life should not be taken on alone. Although you may find it difficult to confide in others about the fear you are experiencing, you will need all the support you can get to challenge this expectation. Once you have allies with you in this struggle, you can connect more clearly to your own unique relationship with your body.

Natalie as a fashion editor for a teen magazine, is caught by the need to be on the cutting edge of style as well as to have the type of body expected for women in her industry. Dana, who you may remember from the expectation "Get a Man," is a teacher from Chicago who deeply desires to settle down and raise a family. She is now married to Shawn and living in Phoenix, but is contending with feelings of isolation in a new environment where exercise and outdoor activities play a greater role than in her former urban setting. Alysia is an accountant from Jackson, Mississippi, who finds it difficult to make distinctions about her body and appearance that reflect her own preferences and identity, not the cultural standards determined by society.

THE COMPARISON TRAP

Natalie loves her job at the teen magazine. She had done well in her journalism major at the University of Virginia, and after working for the local newspaper there, was delighted when she applied and was accepted for this newly created position. It's a good start on her career path, and besides, living and working in New York has always been her dream.

The work is demanding but fascinating. Natalie is thrown into a whirlwind of appointments, interviews, photo shoots, meetings for layouts; she finds she's constantly making decisions about the latest trend, the must-have accessory. At night she attends club openings, dinner parties, art shows. Natalie is running on empty but is afraid that if she cuts back, she'll miss something.

The pace soon wears Natalie down; along with fixing up her apartment, trying to make new friends, and creating a niche for herself at the magazine, she's exhausted. In addition, she finds that she is becoming totally preoccupied with her appearance: Lately, all she can think about is how she looks, especially in comparison to everyone else. Natalie has never been sensitive about her figure before, but now that she's surrounded by all these great-looking, ultra-fashionable women, she finds herself wishing for a slimmer, trimmer, sexier body.

"I can't believe this is happening to me," she says. "Of course I feel better when I look good. I get my hair styled every month and have someone do my makeup regularly. I love keeping up with the latest fashions, and I'm always wearing something new. So, why do I think there's something wrong with me? And if I'm not together about my own appearance, how can I possibly make the right decisions about the fashion spreads I put out every month?"

Natalie is so busy and tense that she begins skipping meals and starts to lose weight. Being *that* thin isn't attractive for her, but the up side is now she looks more like most of the other editors at the magazine, not to mention some of the skinny models she works with. Natalie's new concern, however, is to keep her body firm and toned. Even though her time is already stretched to the limit, she joins a gym where she schedules a daily workout.

It doesn't take long for Natalie to realize she's on a dangerous course. She's worn out physically as well as mentally, and is constantly obsessing about her looks. "Ever since I've been in the fashion world, I compare myself to other women and always come up short," she explains. "I understand that no one can really compete with the photographs of the models and movie stars we publish in the magazine, but I can't seem to protect myself from trying to look like them."

Natalie says she is caught in a "comparison trap" and can't seem to get free of its powerful hold. "I'm always judging myself against the standards of beauty we use in the magazine, obviously a no-win situation," she says. "I feel like a failure because I don't look the way I think I'm supposed to. Sometimes I feel so worthless that I'm scared I'm going to crash and burn."

I suggest that Natalie list the ways this obviously huge problem is affecting her. "It makes me think all the time about how I look," she begins. "I wake up in the morning worried that I'm too fat. Then it seems that I can never get my makeup to look right. Forget about my hair! I try on several different outfits before I decide on one to wear to the office. I hardly eat anything all day, and run off to the gym during lunchtime or sneak a workout in during the afternoon. I find myself cringing when we're doing a photo shoot, more worried about my appearance than how the models look. When I go out with friends, I wonder what they think of me. I notice how people, especially men, watch me and just assume they find me unattractive. All I know is that I want to get off this awful treadmill."

Knowing she wants "off the treadmill" is a first step for Natalie. She begins to pay attention and observe how the feeling of worthlessness brought about by this expectation shows up and what it does to her. She notices when obsessive thoughts, evaluating self-comments, cringes, and shudders occur, then tries to put them aside. As Natalie starts to experience some success in this process, she finds that the worthless feeling subsides.

The next time we talk I ask Natalie at what point she began to know that the context of the fashion world had upped the ante regarding the pressure she was experiencing to Look Good, Be Thin.

"It's not about knowing," she explains. "It's about paying attention to all the specific ways this expectation is able to get to me. You can't fight something that's an idea. You have to see how it really affects you and confront it in a detailed, minute-by-minute way. None of us are really free from the pressure, but knowing it's there helps enormously."

I suggest that maybe this expectation is too big for Natalie to try to challenge alone, and wonder who she could ally herself with in this battle. Natalie surprises me with her idea. "I would like to create a support group with some of the women I work with at the magazine," she says. "We all seem to be in the same boat, and if I tell them about my experience, maybe it will break the ice."

I mention how comparison can sometimes become particularly powerful when women are in groups, and can get them to measure themselves against each other. Natalie considers this and decides to start by speaking to each woman on an individual basis. Then maybe they can find a way to get together and do something they enjoy—like going to a movie after work. Now, Natalie is not only taking action to challenge the expectation Look Good, Be Thin but also engaging others in the process as well.

ENDLESS WORRIES

When we last left Dana, she was teaching in Chicago and had just begun to go out with Shawn (chapter one: "Get a Man"). She was serious enough about the relationship to introduce Shawn to her family and now, a year later, she is twenty-eight, married to Shawn, and living in Phoenix where Shawn is a manager with the local phone company and she is teaching in an elementary school.

Dana wonders if she has found the happy ending she has always dreamed of. She loves her job, and Shawn is supportive and enthusiastic about her desire to become pregnant as soon as possible. They've even bought a house and are beginning to make friends in the local community. Dana thinks she shouldn't have a worry in the world—so what could be wrong?

Yet, seemingly out of the blue, Dana is finding herself becoming overly concerned, even obsessed about her appearance. She remembers feeling the same way when she was going out with Jason two years before she met Shawn. Dana was always self-conscious around him and would check her weight several times a day, convinced that Jason thought she was too fat.

Dana had assumed that all the insecurity about her body and looks would go away once she was in a committed relationship where she felt safe and secure. But in Phoenix, where the weather is warm year-round and there are no bulky winter clothes to hide any extra pounds, she finds she is more focused than ever on her body. At weight-training class, doing nightly laps at the outdoor high school track, riding with the school biking club every weekend, Dana checks out other women and decides she falls short. She even worries how she'll look when she is pregnant, and cringes at having to wear maternity clothes.

Shawn never comments on her body, but the other day she is sure he was looking at her funny when she stepped out of the pool. This so filled her with anxiety that she can't bring herself to ask him if he thinks she has put on weight or is getting wrinkles from the sun. Dana hates it that she's so consumed by this over-attention to her body, but has no idea how to go about tackling what is rapidly becoming a much bigger problem than she could have ever imagined.

Dana says that the pressure from the expectation to Look Good, Be Thin is like an intense agitation, a constant sense of being upset. I ask her how this affects her, and she says, "It makes me think there is something really wrong with me, that I'm not who I should be. I'm filled with doubt, I don't even know who I am anymore. I just know that I don't want to be consumed by these endless worries about how I look. It's not only exhausting, it's a waste of time."

Dana tells me that self-doubt about her appearance has crept into practically every aspect of her life. She worries about what to wear when she wakes up in the morning; she's self-conscious when she puts on her gym clothes and goes to exercise; she's overly cautious about the food she'll eat; and, of course, she's always wondering how others judge her. The only place she feels safe is in her classroom, where the kids just see her as their beloved teacher.

I ask her to consider how the self-doubt has become so big that it's taking over her relationship with her own body. Dana immediately thinks of Shawn, who likes her to look sexy and attractive. But that's not the entire story: She also wants be to be pretty and slim because it makes her feel better.

"I guess what's different now is that I'm living in a really body-conscious environment," Dana says. "Here, everybody is always outdoors and wearing shorts and T-shirts. Many of our social activities revolve around sports and fitness, and there's more opportunity to compare how you look. How can I not think about it?"

When I ask Dana if she thinks her friends may be experiencing the same concerns about the pressure to Look Good, Be Thin, she nods her head in agreement. "The problem is that we never talk honestly about our fear," she explains. "We lie to each other all the time, and know we're lying! If anyone even says, 'I feel so fat,' our automatic response is, 'Of course you're not.' On Saturday, I was shopping with my friend Jessica and I tried on a great pair of shorts that seemed a little tight. She assured me that I looked fine, that Shawn would love how I looked in them. I don't know if she was being sincere or telling me what she thought I wanted to hear."

Dana knows that she is overwhelmed by this problem. She sees how it is making her cut back on eating, even though she is aware she needs her energy for teaching and her eventual pregnancy. She also notices she is increasing the time she spends exercising: She swims more, runs every evening, goes to weight-training class three times a week, and bikes more than fifty miles every weekend. Dana hardly has time to take care of lesson plans and grade papers, let alone spend quality time with Shawn.

Dana tells me that her focus on her appearance is isolating her and keeping her from confiding in anyone how awful she really feels. "I've even kept this from Shawn, who knows that something is bothering me but has no idea what," she says. "Naming the problem self-doubt and seeing all the ways it affects me helps me realize how it's taking over my life. It's much bigger than I thought. I'm neglecting things in my life that are important to me."

I ask Dana what she thinks would happen if she brings the problem of self-doubt into the open. What if she were to break the silence and broach the subject with her friends or Shawn? Even though Dana is sure that would be helpful, she is also skeptical. "How can I expect other people to be honest when I know how hard it is for me?" she asks. "How is it possible to feel safe enough to be sincere with each other?"

I ask Dana why self-doubt is not an issue when she's in the classroom with her students. "That's easy," Dana replies. "I love my work and I know I'm good at it. When I'm in the middle of teaching a lesson, I have the attention of my class and nothing else matters." Suddenly the lightbulb comes on. "Nobody is focusing on my body when I'm teaching, not my students, not my colleagues, not Shawn, and especially not me." She realizes that the key is not to be so consumed by how she looks or thinks she looks. It's a hard task, though, because the *need* to look good is so huge and pervasive.

That week Dana approaches Naomi, a second-grade teacher at the school. "Do you ever worry about how you look?" she ventures cautiously. Naomi laughs. "Are you kidding? All the time. Like every second of the day." Then Dana says, "You know, it seems as if it's perfectly okay to talk to each other about some new diet or what cosmetic surgery we'd like to try, but did you ever notice that we rarely speak about why we are so consumed by our appearance? We never talk about how we really feel, like it's some horrible secret."

Naomi nods in agreement and Dana is relieved. She sees that

Naomi might be open to this kind of discussion. "Do you think it would help if we talk about what really makes us afraid and why we obsess so much about our looks and our weight?" she asks Naomi. "It might be weird, but let's give it a try," Naomi replies.

The secrecy is broken and Dana is no longer a prisoner of self-doubt. There's a beginning of trust between the two women. They can now begin to talk about how self-doubt affects what they eat, how they look, their fitness programs, and their concerns about what others think about them. Listening to each other's stories, they feel less isolated and apart. When Dana asks, "Why is this such a big deal?" Naomi replies: "Look at everything around us. It would take a miracle to escape the pressure to look perfect."

"Well, I want to escape it," Dana says, then surprises herself by adding, "I think it helps to keep talking about the self-doubt rather than all our obsessions."

The pressure to Look Good, Be Thin will never go away, but Dana is making an attempt to confront self-doubt and notice how it comes from all those messages about appearance. For the time being, Dana can share her concerns with Naomi, and one day, hopefully, with Shawn.

Dana is aware that it's important to concentrate on those areas of her life where she feels competent—her teaching, her friendships, her supportive relationship with Shawn. She knows it won't be easy to stop the pressure of this expectation from creating self-doubt, but she thinks she might be able to begin making a distinction between having a healthy body versus a "perfect" one. It's a start, anyway. Plus, she knows she's not alone.

"I WONDER WHAT HE'S THINKING"

At twenty-nine, Alysia has many things going well in her life. She's an accountant in a large firm in Jackson, Mississippi, and lives in the same African-American neighborhood where she grew up. Although her mother lives nearby, Alysia shares a small apartment with a girlfriend. Her job is satisfying, her boss provides her with loads of opportunities for learning, and she has just started a chess club for the children at the local community center. Alysia goes to the gym regularly, rides her bike almost daily, and hikes on weekends with her boyfriend, Marquez.

Alysia's big problem is her ongoing insecurity about her weight. She worries that Marquez thinks her figure isn't right and that she's not well proportioned. "I've always been a large woman so I have to watch myself all the time," she says. "I want to stay in shape and be physically fit, trim, and flexible. It's a constant challenge that can be very frustrating and discouraging."

Alysia put on some extra weight two years ago after she broke her leg in a biking accident. For months she was unable to exercise, not to mention that she began to eat more in an effort to make herself feel better. Alysia was in a relationship at the time of her accident and her boyfriend broke up with her shortly after. The effect was devastating; Alysia became convinced that she was too "fat," and that no man would want to be with her.

When Alysia started going out with Marquez, he assured her that he liked how she looked. They share many of the same physical characteristics: They're both big bodied and slightly overweight. The difference between them is that while Marquez seems comfortable with his appearance, Alysia always thinks she has to do something about hers. She feels extremely pressured to Look

Good, Be Thin, and she gets angry with both Marquez and herself because of it.

"We have our rocky moments," she says. "Even though Marquez never quite comes out and says anything about my weight, I sometimes catch him giving me these funny looks. Or else he'll make a comment about what or how much I'm eating. I usually let it go but it really bothers me. It makes me very insecure and self-conscious about my body."

I ask Alysia if she would call the problem "insecurity." "Yes, absolutely," she says. I then ask her to see if she can identify all the ways this insecurity affects her on a daily basis.

"Well, first off, I know I have to work on getting myself into good physical condition," she says. "I have to go to the gym and watch what I eat—no more fast food or junk snacks. I'm not naturally skinny like some women so keeping my body in a certain proportion is a struggle."

Alysia and I discuss how working out and eating healthy foods can be beneficial. Then I ask her if she's doing this because she wants to or because the insecurity makes her think she has to look good for Marquez.

Alysia considers this question carefully. "I don't make those distinctions," she says. "I don't think of it that way."

The pressure from the expectation Look Good, Be Thin makes it extremely difficult for most women, not only Alysia, to make distinctions about why we do what we do to get our bodies to conform to some standard of beauty. We become blinded to our own idea of what is right for us. All Alysia knows for sure is that she doesn't like feeling insecure about her appearance or her body. She also knows she would like to feel better about how she looks and feels in her body.

I ask Alysia what would happen if she could make those

distinctions. She says, "Well, if I can distinguish between what I want and what I'm supposed to want, then I'd probably be more secure with myself. Maybe I can be more open with Marquez instead of trying to guess what he's thinking."

Alysia realizes that the first step is to notice how insecurity affects her on a daily basis. She starts by paying closer attention to what happens when she feels insecure about her appearance. She notices that all Marquez has to do is look at her in a certain way to make her think he's being critical. She also knows she spends too much time preparing herself before she goes out. She likes looking good, but the insecurity is making her go overboard with her hair, makeup, clothes. Everything has to be just right but never is!

"I often wake up in the morning feeling upset about my body," she confesses. "I never did that as a child but it's getting worse as I get older, especially since my accident. It's just been so difficult for me to get back in shape."

It's important for Alysia to feel good about how she looks—but not to this extreme. Even though she knows Marquez cares about her and means well, she still can't shake off the uncertainty that comes up when they're together. She guesses that the problem isn't him; it's the insecurity that's getting to her. I suggest to Alysia that the very process of naming the problem and seeing how it makes her overly sensitive to her body is allowing her to notice the powerful pressure from the expectation to Look Good, Be Thin. Now she can begin to challenge it.

"I see what you're saying." Alysia responds. "All women have different body types but we are all held to the same physical ideal no matter what our ethnic or racial background is. Diets, fitness programs, fashions all are geared to make you thinner and smaller. For some women, this will never happen no matter what we do. But the point is not to let fear or insecurity take over. We have to face this expectation and decide what we want for ourselves."

Alysia decides she has to talk to someone who understands. Gwen, who is her supervisor at work, has mentored Alysia in her professional life and is like the big sister she's always wanted. Gwen is married, has two small children, and has just been promoted to senior vice president at the firm. She and Alysia also bicycle together when they can. Even though Alysia considers Gwen to be the most together woman she knows, she decides to ask her if she ever worries about her appearance.

"I haven't met a woman yet who doesn't care about how she looks," Gwen tells her. "We all do. I'm glad you came to me because you need to know you're not alone."

Later in the day, as Alysia is thinking about how happy she is that she spoke to Gwen, she realizes they didn't even go into the specifics about how they looked or dressed; they just talked about the worry and the insecurity. Alysia knows that this is the problem she needs to fight, and feels more confident now she knows she has someone by her side. She is taking the steps to make that all-important distinction between how the expectation is pressuring her and what she wants for herself.

WHAT CAN YOU DO?

The tricky thing about the expectation Look Good, Be Thin is that you have to make it a nonissue before you can really face it down. Unlike other expectations, which you can unmask, see for what they are, and reduce their power over you, the appearance expectation is too sneaky, too pervasive, and too ingrained in a woman's beliefs about herself to be easily exposed and expunged. You almost have to ignore it, pretend it isn't there, act like it isn't important, and then reconnect with what is important to you before you can overcome its effects. Easier said than done!

Like Natalie, Dana, and Alysia, the place to start is to recognize the power that self-doubt wields in this expectation, and how it uses comparison, isolation, and a difficulty in making distinctions to get you to think and act a certain way. There are several important areas to pay close attention to:

- How does this expectation get you to notice and compare your body to others?

- How does it influence your eating habits, fashion decisions, and workout programs to control or shape your body according to how you think it should be?

- How does it affect your thinking about yourself as a person?

- Does it interfere with your relationships with people close to you, both women and men?

- Does it get you to feel bad about yourself?

- In what ways does it isolate you, prevent you from talking about the fear and self-doubt, and influence you to speak less than candidly?

- How does it make you act insincerely or get you to doubt the sincerity of others?

It's important to remember that none of the specific activities surrounding the desire to Look Good, Be Thin are necessarily bad. Working out can be an important health factor. Eating appropriate food is known to improve your mood, not to mention your physical well-being. Cosmetic surgery is also an option for some. But remember: This problem is *not* about diet; it is *not* about fitness. It is about self-doubt, and because self-doubt from this expectation serves to disconnect you from your body, deciding on a course of action and making changes can be particularly difficult. Going through the four-step process will show you how to outmaneuver the forceful message of this expectation, and connect to your body with confidence and pride.

RECOGNIZE AND NAME THE PROBLEM

It's probably not very difficult for you to notice all the ways you're concerned about your body. For most women, it is a constant, nagging worry. How do I look? Do these clothes make me look good? Do I need to lose five pounds? Am I attractive? Is my hair okay? Is my makeup right? Am I trim and shapely? Is my body firm?

The questions are endless and, unfortunately, in most cases our answers are always in the negative column. We are not as thin as we want to be. We are not firm enough. Others say we're pretty, but what do they know? Our clothes are not right. Our makeup is out of style. Our hair is wrong. And we never, ever exercise enough. We can't win.

As you begin to notice how this problem is ever present, you will come to understand that you can never measure up to what this expectation demands of you because it is based on unrealistic— and often manufactured—standards of beauty. Its power is often overwhelming, but by giving it a name you can begin to recognize it for what it is. Natalie sees it as a "comparison trap" and "worthlessness," Dana names it "self-doubt," and Alysia knows it as "insecurity." What would you call it?

Pay attention to how this expectation comes up in your life. Since it's always there, recognizing it probably won't be that hard to do. The challenge is to focus on the specific ways it affects you and influences your life. Perhaps you perceive the problem as "shame" or "guilt," or a "sense of failure" or "never being right," or "unworthiness." The important thing is to see that, although the messages are usually about food and fitness, they affect how you think and feel about yourself.

How does this expectation take over? Perhaps like Natalie, it enters your mind in social situations. Or, similar to Dana, it appears when you are exercising or engaged in physical activities. Maybe, like Alysia, it ambushes you when you're with your boyfriend or out on a date.

When you realize the consuming influence of the insecurity brought about by this expectation, you can then acknowledge how dangerous it can be if it takes over your life, ruins your relationship with your own body, or keeps you from making important distinctions. You will then decide you want no part of it. Ask yourself:

- Am I constantly concerned about how I look?

- Do I worry about my eating habits to such an extent that I am not eating healthy foods, am not eating enough, or am overly attuned to the whole process?

- Do I feel bad about myself, not only about how I look but also how consumed I am by thoughts about my body and appearance?

- Do I find myself commenting on food or weight or fitness to an extreme when I'm with my friends?

You may come up with other questions for yourself that will help you see if the problem of self-doubt is taking over your thoughts and choices about staying fit, being thin, and making yourself attractive. Once you can see the specific ways that the problem is affecting you, you are on your way to the next step.

UNDERSTAND AND CHALLENGE THE EXPECTATION

Look Good, Be Thin is an expectation that affects women of all ages. We all want to feel good about how we look; it makes us feel better about ourselves. It is a well-accepted fact that our bodies reflect who we are as persons, and that our identities are inexplicably tied up in how we appear to ourselves and to others. It makes sense, therefore, to be concerned about how you look, what you eat, how you feel about your body, and whether the image you project of yourself fits with what you want others to see.

The problem kicks in when you find that you can no longer distinguish between how the expectation to Look Good, Be Thin pressures you to look and feel and how you really regard yourself. Once you begin to notice the ways self-doubt, insecurity, worthlessness, or whatever you may call the problem influences you, you will be better able to determine the extent of this expectation's influence in your life. Remember, there is nothing wrong in wanting to Look Good, Be Thin: It is only when this expectation takes over and compels you to obsess about your appearance that it becomes harmful. Then you need to challenge it.

Knowing that the expectation Look Good, Be Thin can negatively affect you does not automatically help you escape from its clutches. As Natalie says, "You can't fight an idea." You may go on a diet or work out more or have cosmetic surgery, but these activities won't begin to make a dent in the pressure you're experiencing because they have nothing to do with challenging the expectation. It is only in understanding how this expectation creates a condition of self-doubt that includes comparison, isolation, and a difficulty in making distinctions that you can begin to challenge it.

Look Good, Be Thin works its way into your thoughts and mind by getting you to compare yourself to a standard of beauty that is almost impossible to attain. It then proceeds to isolate you by making you ashamed to admit the fear and insecurity this expectation creates in your life. After a while, you don't know what you really want and are acting in a way that may not reflect your true values and desires.

As you begin to get some distance from the self-doubt Look Good, Be Thin creates, you can unmask this expectation for what it is—an unrealistic demand to look the "right" way. Then, you can discern what it is you want for yourself and return to a more honest and respectful relationship with your body.

Consider the following questions:

• Am I paying attention to what I want to do in my life or am I overly concerned about how I look?

• Am I getting a monthly massage, having a facial every other week, taking a yoga class twice a week, consulting with a nutritionist because I want to be healthy or because the expectation is nagging me to keep up my appearance?

• Are my concerns about my looks taking over other concerns about my life decisions?

• Is this expectation creating comparison, evaluation, isolation, and secrecy? Do I want these pressures in my life?

• Are there times when this expectation is a nonissue? When are they?

Once you begin to distinguish between the reasons why you are making certain decisions or engaging in specific activities regarding your appearance, you will be on your way to challenging the expectation and its power over you.

CONNECT TO WHAT YOU VALUE AND BELIEVE

Connecting to what you value and believe requires you to shut out the forceful and incessant messages this expectation sends, while at the same time recognizing that self-doubt, comparison, and isolation are working together to make the mandate to Look Good, Be Thin a powerful force in your life. You may think it's impossible to ignore the message while noticing its effects at the same time, but the key is to decide what you want to focus on. Although self-doubt will distract you from your talents and what you do best, resist it by attending to what you love and care about.

Natalie is all too well aware of the force of this expectation because of the unrealistic standards of beauty intrinsic to the fashion industry where she works. Even so, her awareness doesn't help her escape the daily demand to Look Good, Be Thin. Only when Natalie sees how the comparison trap affects her in specific and detailed ways can she fight back—and then only by developing relationships with women in her same circumstances.

Like Natalie, can you see the different ways the pressure from this expectation is affecting you and begin to move away from it? How can you escape its power? Natalie doesn't have to leave her job, although she is working in an atmosphere that not only supports this expectation but also promotes it. She knows the messages are there but she decides not to pay attention to them. How can you also do that?

Dana notices the pressure to look good and be thin is a non-issue in her life when she's in the classroom with her students. There she is doing what she likes and feels comfortable with herself and in her body. When Dana is operating in an area of competence, she is confident, not self-conscious. When is this expectation a nonissue for you? Think about the times in your life when you feel self-assured and good about who you are and what you are doing.

As Dana reconnects with herself, she is able to reach out to her friend Naomi. Are there relationships in your life where you feel safe enough to be honest and not worry that you're being judged and compared?

Alysia realizes she didn't have these concerns about her appearance when she was a child but sees they are becoming intense now, as she's older and more aware of the standards for beauty and shape. Awareness of the cultural messages, however, doesn't help her escape from them. The bottom line is that Alysia wants to feel good about how she looks, but not consumed by her appearance.

As Alysia starts to make distinctions about herself, based on what feels right for her, she is able to connect to a time in her life before the insecurity became overwhelming. Can you remember a time or place when you didn't have so many concerns about your appearance? Think of physical activities when you feel comfortable in your body such as dancing, playing basketball, or walking your dog. As you reconnect with these pleasurable feelings, you will be able to begin to distance yourself from the self-doubt created by this very potent expectation. Remember, you cannot fight an idea—only what it is doing to you.

Ask yourself these questions:

• When is self-doubt about your appearance a nonissue in your life? When are you not even thinking about it?

• How are you connected to your own competence and confidence at these times?

• Are there relationships where this expectation doesn't show up? What makes you feel safe and secure in these relationships?

• When does the expectation trigger excessive worry for you, and how does it affect you?

• When you are engaging in certain activities involving eating, exercise, or shopping, notice if you are doing these things for yourself or if self-doubt is directing your activities.

Countering the effects of this expectation and connecting to what you value and believe can only come about by making distinctions about what's important to you, staying close to your own competence, and being comfortable in your body. This is not an easy task, so now—more than ever—you will need allies to support you. Identifying others who can be your allies is key to helping you break the isolation and resist the pressure of this powerful expectation.

SEEK ALLIES AGAINST SELF-DOUBT

The isolation created by this expectation makes it difficult to ask others to join you in your struggle. When the barrier of secrecy is broken, however, it will become apparent that you are not alone, that others have similar experiences and are only too ready to sign up and do battle with you. Natalie reaches out to her colleagues at the magazine; Dana approaches a friend; Alysia confides in a mentor. As each woman begins to reach out, the problem diminishes in its intensity.

Use all your resources in this fight against Look Good, Be Thin. Other expectations can be adapted to your own style, but this one is too cunning an adversary for you to challenge alone. Here's how to help the different people in your life help you.

Helping your mother. In order to consider your mother as a support, remember, once again, that the problem is not about diet or weight, shape or fitness—it is about self-doubt. Your mother wants you to feel good about yourself and proud of your looks. It may be particularly difficult to engage her as your ally, however, because she is also affected by this expectation. She too feels the pressure to be thin, look attractive, wear the latest fashions. Sometimes, you might worry that she is competing with you rather than understanding how the expectation is affecting you.

Choosing your mother to be your ally means that you trust she will be able to understand your predicament. Not all women can have confidence that this is so. Consider carefully how you can invite her to join you in this struggle. How you talk with her is extremely important.

Be honest with your mother:

- Let her know the different ways you are feeling the pressure to Look Good, Be Thin.

- Tell her that you would like her to acknowledge the effects it has on you.

- Explain how you are making distinctions between trying to measure up to certain standards and following your own desires.

- Assure her that she can trust your instincts and judgment, and you want her to know that.

- Confirm that you understand how this expectation affects all women and ask her how it is influencing her.

- Relate specific incidents where she has helped you take care of yourself, and tell her you appreciate her for this support.

- Review together how the pressure to Look Good, Be Thin continues to affect a woman throughout her lifetime.

As you and your mother begin to talk, notice how this expectation affects each of you in different ways. Let her know that her support is important to you in overcoming the isolation and self-doubt that surrounds this expectation.

In addition to engaging your mother in your struggle, you may also want to speak to an aunt or sister or mentor about how you are being affected by the pressure to Look Good, Be Thin:

• Tell her about your concerns and ask if she can identify with them. No doubt she will!

• Find out how she has managed the pressure from this expectation over the years.

• Tell her what you have learned.

• Thank her for how she has helped you; she may not know all the ways she's done so.

When the expectation Look Good, Be Thin tries to overwhelm you once again—and it will—you will have these conversations to fall back on and keep you firm in your resolve.

Helping your women friends. It may be particularly difficult to engage your peers as your allies because of how the expectation to Look Good, Be Thin has contributed to women speaking to each other in less than candid ways about the subject. Sharing your experiences with your friends in a way that breaks the bond of secrecy and frees you to help each other means talking about the self-doubt and your success over it.

• Remind each other that your concerns are not about dieting or working out more but about fear and insecurity and how you want to challenge the expectation that creates these experiences.

• Share stories of success with each other. Give specific examples of how you are able to escape the influence of this expectation and when you find it least powerful.

• Be careful that the language of self-doubt and comparison doesn't sneak into your conversations.

• Let your friends know when you can make a distinction between how you're "supposed" to look and how you feel comfortable in your body.

Whenever a group of women friends get together, comparison and isolation can take hold. Acknowledge that possibility with each other, and share successes you have over self-doubt in this regard. If negative thoughts take over, try to catch yourself and cast these thoughts out of your conversation.

Helping the men in your life. Inviting the men you care about to support you in your battle with this expectation is tricky as their comments can inadvertently feed any self-doubt and insecurity you might experience. Men and women have different issues about appearance, and this can create a set of different realities.

Because the expectation to Look Good, Be Thin gets us to imagine what men might be thinking, we tend to become overly sensitive to their looks and comments. For example, if you ask your boyfriend if you look fat in a certain outfit, do you really believe him? Do you even find yourself becoming angry because you assume he's lying to you or blowing off your concerns? How do you feel when he looks at another woman or comments that a certain actress really looks "hot"?

As you become more comfortable in your own body, you can tell the men in your life what would be most helpful to you as you fight the pressure of this expectation. Even though self-doubt may interfere with your efforts, you should be as honest with them as you want them to be with you. Having an open discussion about your fears and doubts, as you do with your women friends, will open the door to your asking the men in your life to be allies.

GOING FORWARD WITH COMPETENCE

Challenging this expectation will be a lifelong battle. Living a life that fits your own standards of appearance and health, not the ones set by society, is a tough task. The standards set by our culture become our standards, and, as a result, it is often difficult to make distinctions between the two. By overcoming the self-doubt that this expectation creates and casting off its negative effects, you can begin to choose what you want for yourself and find the necessary balance to integrate this expectation into your life with comfort and confidence.

CHAPTER FIVE

Be Popular

"MAKING FRIENDS AFTER college is harder than I thought," observes Lori, twenty-two, a recent graduate of Indiana University where she was a star basketball player. Currently working as a recreational counselor at an Indianapolis youth center, Lori misses the sense of community and support she enjoyed in school. "Sometimes I feel so lonely that it scares me," she says. "I'm starting over and I don't have my teammates to support me anymore."

As Lori is discovering, the expectation "Be Popular" can be extremely stressful for women in their twenties. For the first time in your life, you are expected to make new friends and have a full social life outside the supportive shelter of school and family. If this doesn't happen, you may blame yourself for the problem and assume that something is wrong with you.

You probably hear over and over again how lucky you are to have the opportunity to "do whatever you want" along with marriage and motherhood. Yet, professional success rarely makes up for a lack of intimacy in most women's lives, no matter how old we are, and limited social contacts can stir up feelings of rejection and images of ourselves as failures or losers.

The self-doubt created by the pressure of this expectation can make you feel uncertain about your social skills and shake your confidence in your personal relationships. You know how important friendships are to you, however, so keep in mind that although some relationships come and go, others stay longer and you will always meet new people who can become good friends.

THE DILEMMA

Not so long ago, women used to get married right after high school or college. They left the safety of their family and school, and created a new home with a loving partner. Then, the expectation to Be Popular barely existed because it was assumed women would have a social life centered around their husband's work relationships or their children's activities. Now, as you are probably aware, women are marrying later and are expected to create their own network of friends. This prospect can be very scary, as starting a new job, making decisions, and defining your goals are much easier when you have someone to share them with.

A sense of belonging doesn't necessarily require having a boyfriend or partner but means, more often, knowing you have friends you can trust and count on. Leaving high school is hard enough, but when you leave college you no longer have easy access to ready friendships and organized social activities. Even if you still live in your hometown or college city, or have friends at work, you are facing so many new decisions that the additional pressure to Be Popular can feel overwhelming.

Let's say you find yourself home alone with nothing to do on a Saturday night. You may feel like you have no friends, and that everyone else is out having fun; you may start to think something is wrong with you. The pressure is not so much about hanging out with the "right" crowd like in high school or college, but about believing your friends are there for you, care about you, and understand you. The bottom line is that you need friends more than ever at this time in your life: You want to know you're not alone and have the care and support of others.

Maybe you find that you're trying to fill up your spare time with many different activities, even those you may not like or do well. You may be staying in a relationship that you know isn't right for you just so you don't have to think about what you'll be doing every weekend. If you think you don't have enough friends or find yourself alone more than you'd like, self-doubt may get you to believe that you're unpopular or a social failure.

It's only natural to need and desire friends, as well as a sense of community. Most women treasure their friendships with other women, and find support and sustenance from these relationships. Through our close connections with others we get a sense of the many possibilities of who we can be in our lives. In addition, there is a wonderful security knowing that somewhere in the world you belong to a group of people you feel close to and who are by your side.

You are probably truly on your own for the first time in your life. It's no wonder, then, that the pressure to Be Popular can create such insecurity when there are far too many times you would love to share with a friend but find yourself alone.

Lori is scared she won't be able to make friends once she leaves the supportive environment and close friendships of college; she's afraid she will be lonely without her "team" to back her up. Sylvia comes from an extremely close and loving family, yet leaves them and her boyfriend behind when she moves across country for a new job. In this unfamiliar environment, Sylvia has no idea how to regain a sense of community and begins to question her decision to separate from all that is familiar to her. Natalie, the fashion magazine editor from New York who we just met in the previous chapter Look Good, Be Thin, is now wondering if she—an only child who grew up surrounded by adults— lacks the necessary social skills to make friends and establish meaningful social connections in her life.

MISSING THE TEAM

Lori was a starter on the women's basketball team at Indiana University, and although she would have liked to have gone pro, she wasn't quite good enough. She loves the game and after graduation decides to put her talents to coaching city kids. She takes a job as a recreational counselor at an Indianapolis youth center, deciding that this position will keep her connected to basketball, her passion, and also be an opportunity to meet people who share her love for sports and physical activities.

Lori grew up in a small farming community outside Indianapolis, and high school basketball was her ticket to popularity. The team hung out with each other, traveled all over the state in the school bus, and often planned social activities together. Plus, as the star player, Lori got a lot of acclaim from the fans.

When Lori was ready to apply for college, she was recruited by some of the big basketball schools. She was reluctant to leave Indianapolis but when the University of Connecticut offered her a full scholarship, it was hard to turn down.

Lori was unprepared for how terribly lonely she would feel during her first year at college. Although she liked the other women on the school's basketball team, their camaraderie didn't compensate for her longing to return home and be among her old friends. She wasn't sure why she was uncomfortable in her new environment but somehow felt different from the other students at the school.

At the end of her freshman year, Lori decided to transfer to Indiana University and play basketball there. She soon became a starter, was well liked by her teammates, and got back in her groove. Lori had a social context where she once again belonged.

Now, however, she's scared to death. "I'm starting over, and I don't have my friends to support me anymore," Lori explains. "Life isn't like college, and even though I hope to create some sense of community with my colleagues at work, it's much more difficult than I thought it would be."

Although Lori thoroughly enjoys the kids at the youth center and finds the other counselors pleasant enough, she misses the "team." She feels an emptiness in her life that she never experienced in high school or college, and finds herself scurrying around trying to make and keep social engagements so she won't have to be alone. She works out daily at the local gym and plays on the center's coed basketball team. She goes out every night after work and has her weekend scheduled to the hilt. When Lori is not out with friends, she's on the phone, and when she doesn't have anything planned, she drives three hours to spend time with her parents. She joins an online dating service not necessarily to find a potential partner but to fill up any empty time slots that she might have.

Lori knows she can't keep up this hectic lifestyle, but she thinks she has no option. "I can't bear to be lonely again like I was that first year of college," she says. "It would be too awful."

I ask what it means to be so frenzied about her social life. "I'm always worried about whether or not I'll find myself alone after work or on weekends," she responds. "My schedule is so busy that I don't leave myself time to take care of everyday things for myself. It sometimes gets so confusing that I lose sight of who I am."

When I ask Lori what she would name the problem, she says, "frenzy" or "fear of loneliness." Whatever the problem is, she adds, it's wearing her out.

I ask Lori to review how fear of loneliness and the frantic lifestyle is affecting her. "I don't even know what I want anymore," she says. "I don't have time for myself and feel a constant agitation about whether or not I have every minute covered with something to do and someone to do it with. I'm not getting enough sleep and I'm losing interest in some of the activities I used to enjoy."

Lori stops suddenly with a look of anguish. "All I really want is to be connected with someone," she explains, "but now it seems as if I'm not even connected to myself."

Lori realizes the frenzy has to stop. "I want to have one evening where I can just go home, take a hot bath, read a good book, and go to bed early," she says. Even in her hectic college life with her studies, practices, games, and social activities, Lori remembers that she still took time for herself. "There has to be a balance," she decides. "I want to have friends and create some kind of community where I feel I belong, but not at the expense of my own peace of mind."

I mention that a desire to have others around her is not a bad thing. I then ask her how she thinks this state of frenzy in her life has come about.

"I think it started in middle school," Lori responds. "There's all that popularity stuff, the drama, which continued on through high school. The basketball team was crucial for me because I was sharing what I loved with friends who felt the same way. We all worked for a common goal and were there for each other."

"Maybe there's a clue there for you," I say.

Lori considers my statement. "You mean doing what I love?" she asks.

"Not only that," I explain, "but also noticing the connections you already have in your life."

Lori thinks about how the expectation to Be Popular extends beyond the teenage years. She wasn't prepared for that. Even though the expectation feels less intense now, more like Have a Social Life, it is still demanding.

I remind Lori that the fear and frenzy are taking her away from focusing on what is important to her. "Sometimes I don't even know what I want, at least not on a moment-to-moment basis," Lori replies. "But I can see that it's important for me to ask myself that question. I guess what I really want right now is to have close friends like I did in high school and college. Only then it was easy because I was with my teammates so much of the time."

I suggest to Lori that she look for those moments of closeness—the ones that remind her of her basketball days—but to keep in mind that she is not in school and the rules have changed. She no longer has a seemingly unlimited group of people her own age around her, and must seek potential friends among her coworkers or through social groups she must actively join.

Lori gradually understands that she doesn't have to play by either old or new rules; she has her own rules, which include pursuing what she wants for herself. By doing this, she will meet potential friends she can relate to and feel comfortable with. Lori starts by looking at her relationships at work as well as the activities she enjoys. She decides she likes playing on the coed basketball team with the other coaches from the center and also spending time at the gym after work. The people at both places seem to be on her wavelength, not to mention that the workouts make her feel great and keep her healthy.

As Lori starts to make distinctions between what she wants and what the expectation to Be Popular is telling her, she begins to reconnect to who she really is and what she desires for herself. Lori remembers loving the sense of community she shared with her teammates in high school and college and the support she found from being with people who shared the same values and interests as her. These friends may not be nearby or within easy access right now, but she knows they are an integral part of her history.

Lori decides to create an e-mail list of her "virtual community"—the friends and teammates who helped her become the woman she now is, and who can continue to support her. The first thing she does is contact them and tell them briefly about what her struggle has been. She describes her success over the fear and frenzy, and asks if any of them have had a similar experience. She then encourages her friends to keep in touch with her by e-mail or better yet, visit her if they have the opportunity. She tells them how much she values their friendship and how they continue to be a support to her even though many are far away. Before long Lori begins to get enthusiastic responses from some of her friends. She is surprised at how many write back, and also how many share similar worries and concerns. Lori is determined to keep in touch with them, realizing how important their presence is in her life.

FAR FROM HOME

After several years of working as a legal affairs officer for her local congresswoman, Sylvia, twenty-eight, is promoted to the Washington, D.C., office. This is a wonderful opportunity, as it places her right at the political hub of government, which is what Sylvia has always wanted. It also means, however, that Sylvia will have to leave the San Francisco bay area where her family and boyfriend, Seth, live. She is reluctant to move but knows it would be crazy to turn down such a great job.

Sylvia's parents came to California via Hawaii, where she was born and lived until she was a small child. Sylvia became interested in government through her father's involvement with the city's Chinese-American business community and the group's dealings with different city and state agencies. Deciding that she could be most effective in her career if she had a legal background, Sylvia got her law degree from Berkeley, where Seth is now completing his doctorate in chemistry.

Social relationships are very important to Sylvia and she has confidence in the connections she's created. She has always had a close-knit circle of friends, many of whom are now scattered all over the country pursuing jobs or relationships or both. She has also remained close to her large extended family and frequently spends time with them.

Even so, Sylvia is not prepared for how alone she would feel away from her familiar context. She assumes she would make friends easily, as she had in the past, and doesn't know whether to attribute her isolation to the Washington insider mentality, which is very hard to break through, or having to adjust to an unfamiliar environment, which may just take time. Maybe it's something else she doesn't know about. Whatever the problem is, the loneliness is very real.

Sylvia misses seeing Seth on the weekends. She also misses the lively open-house family dinners her parents have every Sunday. It doesn't help that she's living in a small studio apartment by herself. Nor that she's the newest staff person in the office. She has no connections in Washington—no family, no friends from college who come from the area, nobody except the congresswoman and she's rarely around.

Sylvia makes some attempts to enter the social world of Washington. She goes to staff parties but finds them painful because she feels like an outsider. She tries joining the local gym, but everyone there is quickly completing their workouts, and no one socializes. She joins a book club through the library, but the other members are mostly older women.

The loneliness is so great that Sylvia wants to pack up and go home. She spends most of her evenings on the phone with her family or boyfriend. Although her parents try to understand, they are getting tired of what they describe as her "whining." Seth sounds sympathetic but she knows she's interrupting his work with her constant calls. He tries to keep up with her complaints, but Sylvia can tell he's getting weary of their long, drawn-out phone conversations. Lately, Seth says that he's too tired to do more than have a brief talk, and ends up telling her to not worry, which incenses her, or worse, to deal with it, which makes her feel discounted and misunderstood.

"There must be something wrong with me," Sylvia confides. "I've always been good at making friends and keeping them. I'm very sensitive about what people like and don't like, and I pay close attention to what makes relationships work. So why can't I make friends now?"

I ask Sylvia what it's like to think something must be wrong with her. "It's terrible," she responds. "I'm filled with anxiety. I'm always second-guessing myself, wondering if I said the right thing. I question my every move."

When I ask her to name the problem, she says, "self-doubt" or maybe "second-guessing." She tells me that she doesn't trust anything she says or does and can't understand what she's doing wrong. "All I want is to have friends," she says. "How bad is that?"

"Not bad at all," I say. Then I ask her to consider how second-guessing is affecting her.

"To begin with, I'm lonely and distressed," she says. "I'm always complaining to my parents. I gripe to Seth. I hate my book club. I won't go to parties. I hole up at my computer and don't talk to any one at the office. I go to my apartment after work every day and cry. I just want to go home to San Francisco."

"Going home is always an option," I respond. "But first let's talk about how second-guessing got so big. I agree that moving to a city where you don't know anyone is very tough, but self-doubt and second-guessing seem to be making it even tougher."

Sylvia agrees. "I do value connection and closeness—that comes from my family," she says. "I guess I'm just vulnerable when relationships aren't ready made and available, like it is at home with all my relatives and many of my friends there."

Sylvia remembers how she hated the expectation to Be Popular when she was in middle and high school. "But I had friends there, so I guess I was well liked," she explains. "Now it feels like a dreaded demand. I still want friends, and I should have them. Obviously, there must be something wrong with me if I don't have any."

Then she cautiously adds, "But I'm tough too, you know. So even though it's hard living here, part of me wants to tough it out."

Sylvia then says that she's been thinking it would help if she makes an attempt to keep in closer contact with friends and relatives not only back home but also across the country. "I have free long distance on my cell phone, not to mention e-mail and instant messaging," she says. "Maybe this can hold me over until I get used to the social scene here."

Sylvia wants to call her parents and tell them her plan, but she wants to make sure that self-doubt doesn't cause her to "whine." She wants to make sure she gets the right tone when she speaks to them because her parents have become used to hearing her complain about how lonely she is. She wonders how she can ask them for support without their misinterpreting her need as more than they can offer her.

Sylvia first decides to e-mail Seth to let him know what she's been thinking about. When she sees that he's on-line, she sends him an instant message telling him about her day, her new projects, meeting a legal intern from a senator's office at the cafeteria and making plans to go to a concert together this weekend. Sylvia ends by thanking Seth for understanding how difficult this time has been. He immediately writes back that he's happy for her, that he has all the faith in the world that she'll make her mark in the world of politics, and that knowing her, pretty soon she'll have more friends than she'll know what to do with. Sylvia thinks about their conversation and realizes that by letting Seth know the good things that are happening in her life, he won't feel as pressured to help her, because he won't feel as if he's her sole outlet for support. She hopes that interchanges like this will allow them to be more sensitive to each other and remain close. Sylvia recalls her experiences in past relationships, and how her valuing of closeness helped her be kind and sensitive to others. She wonders how she can reconnect to her values so she can use those skills of kindness and sensitivity to help her now.

Sylvia thinks about the people in her office and realizes that she probably could make friends with some of them. Maybe she can take them up on their offer to spend time together after work. Perhaps she can even become friends with some of the women in her book club.

Sylvia reflects on what it is her parents taught her about the value of intimacy and close connections with other people. Suddenly, she wants to tell them how grateful she is. "Maybe I'm ready to call them and tell them my plans for making my stay here less lonely," she thinks.

Sylvia's brief exchange with Seth, recalling her ability to be kind and sensitive in the past, and the desire to connect with her parents help her face self-doubt and challenge the expectation to Be Popular. Whether she decides to return to California or stay in Washington, the outcome is less important than Sylvia's success over the self-doubt and second-guessing, which will allow her to seek connections and live her social life with greater ease.

I'LL NEVER BE ALONE AGAIN

Natalie, as you recall, considers her position as an assistant editor at a fashion magazine to be her dream job. Living in New York is all that she has hoped for, and she's stimulated by the many activities and diversity of people the city offers. Although Natalie is continuing to struggle to free herself from self-doubt that comes from the pressure to Look Good, Be Thin, at twenty-five years old she believes she's well on her way to a happy existence.

Being popular has never been Natalie's goal. As an only child, she learned to entertain herself and was encouraged by her parents to explore her creative options and artistic talents. Natalie has loved fashion as long as she can remember, and her outfits and sense of style were always a little ahead of those of her class-mates both in high school and college. Although others may have envied her at times, it didn't bother Natalie because having a large group of friends was really not that important to her. She was comfortable with herself and always had one or two girlfriends to spend time with.

Natalie is used to her own company and knows how to take care of herself. Her social life has always met her needs in the past, so she had no qualms moving from Virginia to New York City without knowing a soul. As a result, Natalie doesn't expect the huge wave of loneliness that sweeps over her after several months at the magazine. She finds herself longing to be part of a social circle and to have close friends to confide in.

The pressure from the expectation Be Popular hits Natalie with full force as she struggles with all the adjustments she has to make to accommodate to a new living situation and a new job. Natalie soon begins to feel alone. On top of the demands of the geographical and professional transitions, her struggle with Look

Good, Be Thin takes its toll. It's no wonder that Natalie wants to surround herself with friends and confidantes to help her get through this rough period in her life; what she doesn't understand is why this feels like a pressure.

It's becoming more difficult for Natalie to be around her colleagues at the magazine, most of whom seem to have their social life in place. They're always going to parties, talking about their friends, and keeping happily busy. Their easy intimacy makes Natalie feel even more alone. To make matters worse, she has no idea how to go about creating connections in this strange new place.

Natalie is confused about her reaction to the expectation Be Popular. She never needed a large social circle to be happy before. Why now? Natalie thinks about the few friends she had in high school. They worked together on the yearbook and she still keeps in touch with one of them by e-mail. At the University of Virginia, she joined a sorority so she would have a ready-made group of friends but her only contact with them is from a yearly newsletter. Every once in a while her friend Evan calls from Richmond to find out how her new job is coming. She realizes it is important to her to have close connections. And she wishes she had them now.

Natalie wonders if she lacks the skills to have a meaningful social life. Maybe something is wrong with her, that growing up as an only child caused her to miss out on learning how to develop close relationships with her peers. Natalie begins to think there's a huge deficit in her very being.

When I ask her what she would call this problem, Natalie immediately says she has no social skills. Then she revises her response by saying, "Well, I probably have social skills; I just feel awful at this moment in time."

I ask Natalie to explain what she means by feeling awful. She hesitates briefly, then recites her list. "I overwork so I'll have something to do," she says. "I schedule lunch and dinner meetings with clients so I don't have to eat alone. I go home at night exhausted and just fall into bed."

I remind Natalie about the "worthlessness" and "self-doubt" she experienced with the expectation Look Good, Be Thin. I then ask if the feelings are similar.

"Oh, yes," Natalie responds. "The comparison trap here is that I'm noticing how everyone else seems to have close friends or are paired off while I'm all alone. I'm beginning to realize that I would like to be part of a group, that my own company isn't enough for me anymore. The bottom line is that I would like to be more social."

Even though Natalie doesn't seem to be directly affected by the need to Be Popular, her realization helps her understand that it's exactly the pressure from this expectation that is making her doubt herself and assume she's deficient in some way. Once she reaches this understanding, she is free to reconnect to her desire to have more friends in life and expand her social relationships. As a result, Natalie finds it easier to approach the other women at the office and be more understanding about the social competitiveness around her.

Natalie eventually develops a rapport with Marion, the art editor at the magazine, who always seems to be up and excited about life. Marion comes from a large family in Brooklyn, who instantly include Natalie in all their activities. Marion also has her own group of friends outside the office, and Natalie begins to hang out with them as well. She feels like a whole new world has just opened up to her.

"It's wonderful to know there are new possibilities that can pop up in your life," Natalie says. "I had no idea I could be so outgoing. It's even made my professional life feel more satisfying. Being all alone no longer works for me."

WHAT CAN YOU DO?

Although the expectation Be Popular is not the same for you now as when you were a teenager, the need and desire to have friends is very real. Now that you've left the security of home and college, the pressure to create a social life is complicated by the fact that you actively have to seek out friends and connections. You are in charge of your own social life; if you don't always have something to do and someone to do it with, or if your weekends aren't full of people and plans, you think you must be doing something wrong. Your loneliness is compounded by the fear and anxiety that somehow this is all your fault.

Like Lori, you may find yourself exhausted as you try to re-create the easy camaraderie and intimacy of what you may have experienced during your college years. Maybe you played sports or were involved in theater; perhaps you were active in student government or a volunteer group. Now that you're out of school, these options for creating community probably seem less available and more diffuse. The world is suddenly too big.

You may try to pare it down by joining a gym where you swim regularly. You may take a pottery class, join a hiking club, enter into interesting chat rooms on the Internet, or sign up for an on-line dating service. Perhaps you're just thinking about all this but mostly find yourself coming home from work and calling your parents or college friends, or sitting and watching television as you feel lonely and worry that something is wrong with you.

You may have moved to a different city, like Sylvia, and don't know where to begin meeting people. Even if you have confidence in your ability to make friends, starting new relationships at work is not as easy as it was in college. You may be trying what you know has worked before, but the situation has changed. Then there was a larger pool of candidates available to form relationships. Not only were they closer to you in age, chances are they shared many of your interests. But now you feel like you no longer know the rules. People are of all ages and seem to be from such different backgrounds. You don't know where to start. You feel like a failure because you find yourself wanting to go back home.

Maybe you identify with Natalie, and being popular has never seemed like a heavy-duty expectation. However, adjusting to a new job can be more difficult than you imagined. Everyone seems to know each other, and you feel like you're elbowing your way in. It's easy to begin to blame what you imagine is a lack of social skills for being alone. You're ripe for the onset of self-doubt and its consequences.

RECOGNIZE AND NAME THE PROBLEM

Leaving home, graduating from college, or taking a job in a new city can trigger an experience of self-doubt around the expectation to Be Popular. Suddenly you are in new surroundings, out of your comfort zone, and away from your family and friends. Understandably, you are probably lonely.

Once again, begin by noticing your experience and think about what you might name the problem. You may be feeling uneasy, agitated, irritable, or just plain unhappy. For Lori, the problem is "fear of loneliness." Sylvia names it "self-doubt" and "second-guessing." Natalie calls it "feeling alone" or "feeling awful." Whatever you name it, it usually has to do with how it gets you to doubt yourself in some way. Pay attention to how the problem affects your desire for closeness, for connection, for intimacy, for community, and for belonging; notice how it makes you think you must somehow have "gotten it wrong."

Be as specific as you can about what this problem does to your life. Lori ends up having no time for herself; her frenzied, hectic lifestyle keeps her on the go to the point where she stops thinking about whether or not she even wants to do what she's doing. Overactivity and exhaustion become constant in both her work and personal life. Sylvia finds that second-guessing causes even her closest relationships to suffer. Her parents think she's whining, her boyfriend feels pressured, and nothing seems to work to relieve the loneliness. Natalie believes she's not likeable. The awful feeling makes her think she is destined to be alone and that she will never have the necessary social skills to create a life of connection with others, a community of friends.

What does self-doubt, or whatever you have named the problem, do to you?

- Is it getting you to focus on how difficult the transition is that you are experiencing?

- Does it make you forget the friends you already have and the connections that are readily available to you by e-mail or cell phone?

- Do you find yourself complaining all the time about your lack of social activities?

- Are you making plans to be with someone even though you really don't want to spend time with that person?

- Do you question your ability to make friends, be with people, and be socially acceptable?

- Are you wondering if your past history of making friends is all just a sham?

- Is self-doubt making you think you are not likeable?

Look carefully at your answers to these questions to see how the effects of self-doubt may be wreaking havoc with your sense of self as a social being. As you recognize how self-doubt is blinding you to the connections you already have, to the possibilities that exist in your life, and to your proven talents to make new friends, you will probably decide that it is not for you.

The expectation Be Popular is grounded in a well-accepted belief that people are not meant to be alone, that we are social beings and need to interact with others to live well. Many experts believe that an ability to form attachments with others is the key to our overall health. Emotional intimacy is a necessity, but when it takes the form of an expectation, the pressure can make you wonder if you will be able to measure up. By overcoming the self-doubt that comes from this expectation, you can take the next step.

UNDERSTAND AND CHALLENGE THE EXPECTATION

The lessons you learned about relationships as you were growing up are critical to your survival. Your parents are your first teachers, and then your siblings show you how to negotiate the territory of working things out. Your next contacts are with your preschool and elementary school classmates, followed by your friends from the murky waters of middle school and high school where the rules became more exacting.

You probably still have some connection with your friends from those growing-up years. Many people say: "My best friend is someone I've known since the third grade," or "I get together with some classmates from college every year." It's no surprise that these relationships are often the most enduring, as those connections were made when there was a wide circle of possible friends readily available to you over a long and continuous period of time.

Although most of us go on to make new friends throughout our lifetime, it's difficult to have such a long-term perspective when you are in your twenties. You have only recently left the company of your peers, and even if you still have friends from college or earlier, they probably are not so easily available. You may have moved to a new city or taken a new job. Your time is limited and there are few people your age or with your interests in your immediate circle. Yet, the need to have friends is still constant, and the expectation to make sure you have people to hang out with, someone close to talk to, a date on the weekend, not to mention myriad other social activities, is constantly wearing on you.

The expectation to Be Popular—although it probably doesn't get spoken of that way—is silently making itself known. The first and most important task, once you have looked self-doubt in the eye, is to understand that the pressure you have been feeling is coming from this expectation. By making this mandate visible, you can face it for what it is. It's wonderful to have a group of close friends you can count on. But the pressure to make it all happen in a particular way and right now is terrible.

How can you challenge what the expectation to Be Popular is doing to you? Lori realizes that the frenzy and fear is making her unsure about what she wants from her social life. She also sees that she doesn't have to play by the rules she learned in middle school, but can create her own rules and pursue what she loves. Lori remembers wanting to join the basketball team in high school and college so she could be with people with whom she had something in common. She knows she can find friends with similar interests to hers once again, allowing her to begin to make distinctions between what she wants and what this expectation is telling her to do.

Sylvia has always hated the expectation to Be Popular. During her middle and high school years, she was able to hold her own and have friends without acting petty or unkind to others. When she sees what second-guessing is doing to her now, she understands how this expectation has become a dreaded demand in her new life outside of a familiar context. She also realizes she is resilient and can resist the pressure of this expectation by noticing the connections already available to her as well as expanding her circle to include new friends of all age groups.

Natalie is blindsided by the expectation to Be Popular. She had never before been consumed by the need to make friends; she was comfortable with herself and at ease with the social life she had. A new city, new job, and noticing how others around her seem to have close connections make her doubt her own social skills. Once Natalie realizes that the pressure she's experiencing is coming from the expectation, she can face it and decide what she wants to do. She then recognizes that what she really wants is to have more friends, and becomes free to seek a richer social life.

As you clear away whatever anxiety and stress you are experiencing in your life to make friends, be busy socially, and work at your relationships, notice that this pressure is coming from the expectation to Be Popular. By exposing the power of this command, you can see how it may be affecting you in harmful ways and will be ready to challenge it. You may then find yourself doing the following:

- Realizing you can create your own rules for relating to others.

- Paying attention to the connections you do have: a colleague at work, a new acquaintance from your book club, someone at the theater class you're attending.

- Joining a group or organization and knowing there will be people there who share your interests.

- Deciding that your relationships don't all have to be with people your own age exclusively, that friends in different age groups might open new possibilities for seeing life in different ways.

- Finding a way to stay in touch with relationships you have had for a longer time using e-mail, phone calls, and reunions when you're in the same geographical vicinity.

- Making distinctions between how you want to create close connections in your life and what the expectation to Be Popular is making you believe.

As you get better at understanding how this expectation is affecting you and notice the ways you can challenge it, you will also become aware of those moments of closeness when you really connect with someone, even for a brief period. You will cherish those times, because they will help you acknowledge yourself as a social being, a person who wants intimacy in her life and can create lasting friendships. Then you will be ready to take the next step of reconnecting to your own history of relationships.

CONNECT TO WHAT YOU VALUE AND BELIEVE

A particularly negative effect of the expectation to Be Popular is that the self-doubt it creates not only disconnects you from others but also disconnects you from yourself. Reversing the effect, as we have seen before, means getting free of self-doubt so that you can reconnect with yourself, your own values and beliefs, and your own history of competence in relationships. You can then begin to create the social context you want for yourself.

You might start by remembering the values of connection that your family holds. Maybe they are implicit and subtle. Lori, for example, may have learned from her parents that belonging to a team would help her find easy access to friendships. Perhaps your parents' values are clearly expressed, as in Sylvia's family, where closeness and intimacy are dearly treasured. Natalie, on the other hand, may have been included and involved with her parents, but had no siblings to work things out with and easily became her own company. Still she finds it important to have others in her life. Think about some of the values you grew up with.

- Remember early messages you received about how to relate to others.

- Recall connections that your parents created for you and the ones that lasted.

- Think about a friend from your childhood days and what she or he brought to your life.

• Recount the many things you have learned from the relationships you've had throughout the years.

• Think about the friends you've kept contact with, and list the reasons you want to keep them in your life.

• Wonder about those friends you have lost contact with and think of any with whom you'd like to reconnect.

Now ask yourself how your values affect your current friendships.

• If you were to ask all your friends what it is about you that makes you a good friend to them, what would they say?

• Make your own list of what makes you a good friend to others and compare it to the one that came from your friends.

• For each of your relationships, think about what particular joy or richness they bring to your life.

• Remind yourself of who you go to for what, and how each of your friends meets a different need or desire.

As you notice your responses to the above list, think about what your personal manifesto of friendship includes, what is important to you, what you learn from others, and what you bring to relationships. Recall your skills in creating connections by reflecting on your past history of making friends. Consider if these relationships were based on personal interest, easy access, life coincidence, or "chemistry." Ask your parents to tell you about how you made friends as a child and think about why your relationships with old friends have endured over the years. How would the friend you have had the longest remember your early history? What would the people you have kept in your life know and say about how you sustain relationships?

As you reconnect with your desire to have others in your life, think about what you consider to be a close connection. Remember how you like to make contact with others, what works best for you in a friendship, and how others respond that allows you to keep the closeness intact.

Natalie found a new life of companionship when she became friends with Marion. What vistas are open to you through new relationships you have made or are currently making? What are you learning about yourself that delights you?

As you connect with your values and beliefs, think about what you like about yourself and wonder how you can help others appreciate that about you too. Having others in your life who care about you and you can count on—and who in turn can count on you—is both necessary and desirable.

SEEK ALLIES AGAINST SELF-DOUBT

Allies are a very special type of friend. They are those who see you, appreciate you, and support you, no matter what. They are often your "best" friends, people you are in continuing contact with or voices from your past who may no longer be available to you.

You may be asking yourself how it's possible to seek out allies to help you challenge the expectation to Be Popular when self-doubt is telling you that you have no friends and maybe are even incapable of making them. For example, Lori is unable to see the connections she already has. Sylvia's parents think that she's complaining and Seth seems annoyed by what he considers her constant need to connect with him. Self-doubt convinces Natalie that she doesn't have any social skills and doesn't know where to learn them.

As you reconnect with what you know and believe, however, you will start to recognize the relationships in your life that are already in place; you may even notice that you possess the necessary skills to make and keep friends. When this happens, you can begin to consider people who might be candidates for you to list among your allies.

Many women don't usually think of their mothers when they consider allies because they are more focused on their own peer group. You may find that even though your mother wants you to have friends, she is not especially practiced in acknowledging the distress you are feeling about your social life. Because she is full of worry for you and finds it difficult to know how to support you, you might assume that she doesn't care what you are going through. On the other hand, she may be asking so many questions about your social life that you feel as if your privacy is being invaded. As a result, you may not trust your mother to know what to say—or not say—and perhaps she won't. Here's what you can do to help her.

Helping your mother. We all want to have close friends in our lives, and undoubtedly your mother has learned that although her husband is her partner and may be her biggest supporter, sometimes she wants to turn toward her women friends for an appreciation and understanding that comes from a woman's perspective. She will know that about you too. She wants to be your confidante, your advisor, your ally. If you help her do that, she will be grateful and you will know you always have someone to count on.

Your mother will also be sensitive to your need to have

friends among women close to your own age who will better understand what you deal with on a daily basis. Let her know things such as the following:

- Who your friends are and some of the activities you share with them.

- How important your friends are to you, and that you know she would understand that from her own experience.

- What you appreciate about all you have learned from her as you negotiate your relationships.

- What you share with your friends about your closeness with her.

- That there are some things you may not want to share with her.

- Mostly, how you have overcome self-doubt to reconnect with your own ability to form relationships and that you know she will be glad to hear of your success.

Your conversations with your mother should reassure her that you are confident in your ability to have supportive relationships and that you don't want her to worry about you as you continue to go forward in your life. You will want, however, to turn to her for advice and support on occasion.

Sometimes your mother may not be available to be your ally. She may no longer be living or is occupied with her own life and relationships. Maybe she has trouble understanding what you are going through. Even so, keep in mind that she cares for you and that you can keep her close as an ally in your heart.

You may have other friends, nearer to your mother's age than yours, who have mentored you and who you trust. This connection has a different quality than your friendships with women who are your peers. To help your aunts, teachers, mentors, and coaches be your allies, let them know about that difference.

Your women mentors may have experience in a particular area that you don't have. Although they probably can't enter into your contemporary culture in the ways that your friends can, they will be freer from those influences and how they affect you. Think what you may gain from the women mentors in your life:

- A perspective with a longer view than you could possibly have.

- Knowledge that fads and interests come and go, and that you can pick and choose new interests and people to share them with you.

- An understanding that you will always be able to make new friends in your life.

- An appreciation of long-standing relationships and that friends can be people of all ages.

Helping your women friends. A good place to start in creating an ally group is to remember friends from your past: a childhood acquaintance from elementary school who you call when you go back home; a friend from high school who you get together with when she's in town; or a college roommate who e-mails you regularly. They, undoubtedly, also have experience with the pressure to Be Popular, and if they have had their own success over self-doubt, they can readily understand how this expectation is affecting you. These friends can be the first among your allies, as they can truly get what you are going through.

As you begin to be more confident in your knowledge that you can create new friendships in your life, you can be on the lookout for new allies. As time goes on, you can then share your experience with them about how you have overcome self-doubt and challenged the expectation Be Popular.

As always, it's important to share your successes rather than focus on your struggles with self-doubt. Most of us have limited patience for listening to story after story about the insecurity of others; it triggers our own experiences and saps our energy to help. Allies are much more apt to come to your defense when you have a clear plan for victory and can tell them what part they can play. They are no longer at loose ends and know exactly what their role can be.

- Be clear about what you need and want from your friends and that the help they give is important and significant.

- Be very explicit with your old friends about how they have helped you in the past and how grateful you are that they are in your life.

- Celebrate your victory over self-doubt together with friends you trust and who care for you.

- Acknowledge their status as allies.

When you are clear with your friends about how they are also your allies, you'll find your relationship with them will feel more solid and the community you create will be more secure. This community may also include some of the men in your life.

Helping the men in your life. Once your social group is in place it will undoubtedly include both women and men, and not just a man who is a boyfriend or husband. Some of these men can also qualify as allies. They may not know that you have struggled with the expectation to Be Popular. In addition, the men in your life most likely have no idea about your experience of self-doubt. How can you invite them to become allies?

• Let them know how important they are to you.

• Discuss with them how they manage the expectation Be Popular and if it works differently on men than it does on women.

• Remind them how closeness and intimacy mean a great deal to you.

• Ask them to celebrate with you and your women friends as you continue to create community together.

Perhaps Lori could talk with some of the men, as well as the women, who are on her coed basketball team. Sylvia could consider inviting several people from the congresswoman's staff, both men and women, to her place for dinner. Natalie might call her father one evening and ask him to help her think about how she made friends in her life.

In an effort to call forth allies to support you in your quest for friendship and to challenge the expectation to Be Popular, you will want to extend your social net as wide as possible and notice the different possibilities available to you. Self-doubt often blinds you to what might be options for connections. As you see more clearly, continue to open the door for new friends and allies.

GOING FORWARD WITH COMPETENCE

Overcoming the self-doubt that comes from the expectation to Be Popular is no small task, as this expectation is grounded in a very real need: having close relationships with family, friends, and community. Pay attention to the qualities you possess that make you a good friend; remember also the friendships from your past that you want to hold fast in your life and continue to look for the possibilities of creating new and rewarding relationships in an ongoing way. Knowing that people care about you is priceless.

CHAPTER SIX

Leave the Nest

LORI, THE BASKETBALL star from Indianapolis who you met in the last chapter, "Be Popular," decides to leave her job as a recreational counselor at a youth center so she can join her friend Julia in Miami and find work there. Lori believes it's time to strike out on her own, away from what seems familiar and routine. She's worried about how to afford the move, however, so she asks her parents if she can stay with them until she can get her financial situation straightened out. Now that Lori finds herself back in her childhood bedroom, however, she wonders if she's made a big mistake.

"I can't believe I'm twenty-five years old and still living at home," Lori says. "I should be out on my own already. Why did I think I could come back here?" Lori is caught in an in-between space—that very difficult transition when you leave a place you know and move toward a place you don't.

Does Lori's experience sound familiar to you? Many young women live at home with their parents after college or, like Lori, following an initial experience of living on their own. So, although it may seem natural and important to have a safe space where you can "transition" to an independent life, self-doubt too often sets in and pushes you to go forward before you are really prepared to do so.

The expectation "Leave the Nest" requires that you separate from the familiar context of home and build a life of your own. Your goals are most often specified for you: a college degree in a recognizable field, a quick choice of profession, living away from your parents as soon as possible, and eventually establishing a family of your own. You are expected to achieve these goals in a highly compacted time frame, forcing you to make immediate choices about your life even if you're not quite sure what you want or what path you should be taking.

Because Leave the Nest involves figuring out a series of tough issues, you may find yourself confused or almost paralyzed with indecision. These questions are most often tied to the question of where you will live. Should you get married or be involved in a significant relationship? What career path is best to follow? How can you support yourself? Which city or town do you want to live in? The slightest hitch in any of these areas can topple the tower you're building and lead to the appearance of self-doubt, making it difficult to think about, let alone act upon, what you really want to do.

Growing up and leaving home means negotiating all those decisions that lead toward independence as well as creating new experiences that work for you. In the twenty-first century, a woman's place is wherever you want it to be, although to get there you may have to go through one or more transitions, including living at home, remaining in your college town, or sharing an apartment with a best friend. As you begin to overcome the self-doubt created by the pressure to Leave the Nest, you will find that establishing your own independence is directly related to the relationships that sustain and nurture you.

THE DILEMMA

What are the hallmarks of independence? Because this expecta-tion involves so many changes, you may not know when or if you have truly "left the nest." You graduate from college, you get a job, you live in your own apartment, you try to support your-self, you have a steady boyfriend, you break up, you live at home for a while, you get engaged, you change jobs, you move to an-other city, you go back to graduate school, you lose contact with old friends and make new ones along the way, you travel to and live in another country, you live with a boyfriend or partner, you get married, you start your own family.

There are many events that can trigger a feeling of insecurity and force you to question whether you're making decisions that will lead to the independent life you know you want. In the pro-cess, the pressure from the expectation Leave the Nest may influ-ence you to cut yourself off from people you love and care about.

For example, you may think you can no longer turn to your parents for help and feel that their advice is intrusive and judg-mental. They may ask you: "Aren't you overqualified for your job? Have you taken care of your car registration? Should I co-sign on your lease? Why did you pick *this* apartment? Are you sure you can afford cable TV?" Not wanting to hear what may feel like a criticism of your choices, you may begin to limit your contact with your parents and find yourself jealously guarding your personal space.

As a result, you may find yourself at a loss about who to turn to when you run into roadblocks or need advice about the decisions you face about your future. You assume you have to figure out your problems immediately and on your own or you'll end up with a barrage of unwanted advice. Flying solo, family and friends who are natural allies may seem more and more distant, and you may begin to feel more alone than ever.

Self-doubt from Leave the Nest can easily make you forget what you value and what gives you strength and comfort—staying connected to what you know as well as seeking out allies. Appreciating and respecting supportive relationships in your life allows you to be flexible and remain confident in your ability to Leave the Nest, and to create the life you want while remaining connected to the people you love.

Lori has moved back home to live with her parents while she prepares for her move to Miami. Although she is aware that this is a temporary arrangement, Lori is in an in-between space, leaving her previously independent life and going toward a new, unformed one. Maria, who achieved financial independence and successfully challenged the expectation "Make It on Your Own," is now twenty-six and married to Alfredo. They are living in a house with a separate living space for Maria's mother, and although Maria is pleased with this arrangement, she soon finds herself questioning if she is too emotionally attached to her mother. She begins to doubt if she has really "left the nest" and is truly establishing her own independence. Melissa, the Los Angeles writer from the chapter "Have a Career," is feeling frustrated and stuck. Now twenty-seven, she wonders if she is holding back because she's afraid to leave the security and safety of her friends and community, and questions if she can make changes in her life without losing these important connections.

THE IN-BETWEEN SPACE

After three years at the recreation center, Lori is ready for something new. Lori's degree is in communications, so she's considering looking for work in a public relations firm or going back to school for a master's degree in business. Although Lori's one venture out of state didn't go well—she left the University of Connecticut after her freshman year and transferred home to Indiana University—Lori learned a great deal from that experience. She is also feeling much more socially assured after having successfully challenged the expectation Be Popular.

When Lori receives an e-mail from her former basketball teammate Julia, now working as a translator for an international firm located in Miami, she's intrigued by Julia's suggestion that Lori join her there. Julia writes that the weather is great, the social scene relaxed, and the sports activities are nonstop. Lori wants to explore new possibilities, and she thinks that rooming with Julia can be a starting-off place for new experiences, new friends, and a new life. The problem is money: All of Lori's salary goes to cover her living expenses, and her savings can barely cover her airfare to Florida, let alone moving costs.

Lori thinks it would help if she can decide what to do with her life without worrying about paying her bills. Early in the spring, Lori gives notice at her job and on her apartment, packs up her things, and moves back home. Her parents seem pleased with the idea, and while her friends are sad to see her go, they give her a big going-away party where they toast her past success and the new adventures that lie ahead.

Lori has always been close with her parents, who have encouraged her to be independent since she was a little girl. She respects the long hours they work at their flower supply business several hours from Indianapolis, and is more than happy to help them out in the greenhouses during their busy season. Lori pitches in right away while also spending a great deal of time checking out job possibilities and graduate schools in Miami.

As the weeks go by, Lori begins to wonder why she is making this change. Although she was getting bored at her job, she liked her life in Indianapolis and had great friends. Lori soon begins to have doubts about her decision: She's left something safe and secure behind, and has no idea what is going to happen next.

"Why did I come back home?" she asks her parents. "I love you dearly, but I need to be on my own. I feel like a child again, even though I know you don't treat me like one."

Lori's parents are sympathetic. They tell her it will all work out, that this is a transition time—which is always rough. They encourage her to keep going forward, and although she knows they mean well, Lori reacts to their supportive words with gloom and doom. "This is awful," she says. "My life has come to a dead halt. I should never have left my job."

Lori begins to feel very isolated. She spends more and more time on the Internet, e-mailing her friends and joining different chat rooms. She misses being with people her own age and is convinced that she has made a wrong turn somewhere along the road. Self-doubt is taking over her life once again.

Lori calls Julia in Miami and shares her confusion. "I'm beginning to think I'm really stupid and learned nothing from the past," she confides. "By now, I should know how important my friends are to me. And what do I do? I just up and leave them all."

Julia listens carefully, then tells Lori how she too was confused and anxious about whether or not to leave home and move halfway across the country. "That's a relief," Lori responds. "I thought it was only me. So how did you finally manage to make it through the maze and decide what you want to do?"

Julia laughs. "It wasn't easy, that's for sure," she says. "I wasn't sure what was going on, but when I thought about it, I realized I was feeling a lot of confusion and was questioning every move I made. It dawned on me that my problem was more about self-doubt than about my desire to be on my own."

Lori resonates with Julia's experience. She begins to understand that she too is experiencing self-doubt, and decides to make a list of all the ways it is affecting her. She e-mails the list to Julia to see if it's similar to her experience.

"I think I'm stupid and very, very wrong," she writes. "I'm forgetting what the past lessons of life are. I know I need friends, and here I am in what feels like exile. I love my parents, but I'm even beginning to resent their encouragement. I'm starting to hate my life."

When Julia responds right away with, "Lori, that doesn't sound so good," Lori sees how ludicrous her situation is. Self-doubt is making her forget what her goals are: to get a job in public relations, maybe go to graduate school, and to have new and exciting experiences. Although she longs for the comfort of her old friends and welcomes the support of her parents, Lori is ready to leave this in-between space behind and move forward.

Lori begins to realize that although she is particularly vulnerable to self-doubt at this time in her life, she wants nothing of it. Nor does she want any of the pressure from the expectation Leave the Nest. Lori decides to take a break and spend a week with Julia in Miami. This way, she'll have a more realistic knowledge of the situation there to help her make more informed decisions about work and school. Lori is clear that she wants to take this next step, and self-doubt is not going to stop her.

TOO CLOSE?

Once Maria wrestles down the expectation "Make It on Your Own" and realizes she can be an equal partner with Alfredo, she easily makes the decision to get married. Maria and Alfredo combine their savings to buy a small home with a separate living area for her mother so they can continue looking after her. Maria feels more secure that her mother is living in the same house with her, but is also pleased that she and Alfredo have a space of their own.

Maria knows that Alfredo is fine with the arrangement. He also believes it's the responsibility of children to take care of their elderly parents, as his younger sister is living with and caring for their mother. Maria and Alfredo are comfortable sharing the up-keep of their mother-daughter house and consulting with each other on all of their financial decisions.

Maria continues to enjoy her work at the geographical survey firm. Not only that, she and Alfredo have decided to start a family, so she is trying to get pregnant. Maria loves the easygoing life she and Alfredo have created together, and that she can share so much with her mother.

"Sometimes my mother and I talk for hours on end when I get home from work or over the weekend," Maria says. "We also cook together and she helps with some of the household chores.

Mom says that she can hardly wait until I start having babies so she can take care of them, and I'm glad because it will free me up to continue working."

Lately, however, Maria is beginning to wonder if something isn't quite right. This feeling began when a new acquaintance expressed surprise at Maria's living arrangements, asking her if she considered her mother's close presence an invasion of her privacy. Even though Maria doesn't think of their relationship as overly involved, the comment makes Maria wonder if, in fact, she may be too emotionally connected to her mother.

"I like being able to take care of my mother and having her around," she says. "And it's not a one-way street. My mother is also a great source of comfort and help to me." But Maria finds herself starting to think she may be doing something wrong, that maybe she's not spending enough close time with Alfredo, and she soon begins questioning why she is sharing a house with her mother at all.

Fortunately, Maria can see that what is happening to her is similar to the second-guessing that bothered her when she struggled with her desire for financial independence. Here comes self-doubt, she tells herself, only this time it has to do with whether having her mother around is somehow interfering with her independence. "I wonder if I'm kidding myself," Maria says. "Maybe my mother should have her own place, and I could pay her expenses. We could still see each other but not all the time like it is now. Then maybe I'd share more with Alfredo instead of always turning to my mom."

As Maria considers different alternatives, she not only questions herself but also feels intense guilt. She cherishes her close connection to her mother, and when she thinks about living apart from her she feels bad. "Why is it so wrong to want to share my life, my thoughts and feelings, and even my house with my mother?" she asks herself.

The ensuing confusion begins to affect Maria in different ways. She finds herself becoming irritable with her mother, criticizing almost everything she says. Although they have always been honest and open with each other, now all her mother has to do is express an opinion and Maria wants to contradict her. Maria begins to avoid her mother, coming home late from work, not wanting to eat the wonderful meals her mother cooks, and spending most of the evening in her room.

During the family get-togethers on weekends, Maria hangs out with her brothers and sisters or plays with her nieces and nephews, leaving others to entertain her mother. Alfredo begins to notice how Maria is staying clear of her mother, but when he points this out to her Maria dismisses his concerns. Soon she and Alfredo are nitpicking and finding fault with each other. At work, one of Maria's supervisors asks her if something is bothering her.

Maria is confused and goes to her oldest friend, Elena, for advice. "I don't know what's come over me," she confides. "I love Mom and have always enjoyed doing things with her. Now I find that I don't even want to be around her, let alone take care of her. I feel so guilty, like I'm a bad daughter."

Maria explains how the doubts about her relationship with her mother surfaced when she was asked about her mother's sharing a house with her and Alfredo. "I'm even thinking of moving her out to her own place or asking one of my brothers or sisters to take her," she tells Elena. "But that just feels wrong—I like having my mother near me."

While talking with Elena, Maria remembers that in the past, naming the problem and reviewing what it was doing to her was extremely helpful. She clarifies: "I think my irritability is coming from self-doubt, not my mother," she says. "Remember how confused I was about whether I could marry Alfredo and still feel financially capable? Well, now self-doubt is making me question my relationship with my mother, one of the most important people in my life. Not only that, I'm irritable with my husband, my colleagues at work, and my friends."

Elena nods sympathetically. "There's nothing wrong with your wanting to be with your mother and helping her out," she reassures Maria. "You're still independent. You have your own life. You and Alfredo have your own space and your own plans."

Elena's words help Maria to get some clarity on the problem. She sees that she has been affected by the pressure from the expectation to Leave the Nest, which often means leaving home and cutting all ties with your parents. It's a difficult distinction to make, but Maria knows she can be independent and also stay close to her mother.

"Self-doubt made me forget that having my mother in my life is something that's very important to me," Maria says. "You're right, Elena. I can stay connected to my mother, be close to my husband, and be independent at the same time."

WHAT'S AHEAD?

Melissa is pleased with her freelance writing career but is afraid she's taking the easy way out by not pursuing any job offers that would mean leaving Los Angeles. California feels more like her real home than Colorado ever did, and she loves her group of friends whom she now considers her family. "But how could I ever move from here after I've created such a full life for myself?" she wonders. "And do I really want to do that?"

Melissa has a wonderful apartment close to the beach; her roommate Alex is like the brother she's always dreamed of; and she recently adopted a cat that she adores from the local animal shelter. Her social life is rich and varied, and she has registered for a class in media communications at the local arts center.

"So why do I feel old and jaded at my young age?" Melissa asks Alex, only half kidding. "Lots of my former classmates from college are envious of the position I'm in. They see me as independent and financially self-sufficient, getting bylines every week, having wonderful friends, and living near the ocean. It's true my life is great, but I keep thinking there's more out there and somehow I'm too afraid to take the next step."

Alex suggests that Melissa may be ready to get married and settle down. "Are you and Chris serious about your relationship?" he asks.

Melissa smiles. "Not exactly. Yes, I do want to get married and have kids someday, but that's not what's bothering me. I think I should be able to be on my own more and not depend so much on my friends. Then I ask myself what's so wrong with wanting to be with people you care for. Isn't that more important than a great career or lots of money?"

Melissa questions why she can't be content: Is she just destined to be always a little dissatisfied and unsettled? Yet, she believes there's some other opportunity for her that she wants and needs to access, even though she's reluctant to go look for it.

The expectation to Leave the Nest is beginning to exert pressure on Melissa, creating the familiar feeling of self-doubt she recalls so clearly from her struggle with "Have a Career." Melissa finds herself worrying about her choices. She wonders if she's wasting her time—and talent—freelancing instead of looking for a full-time job. She doubts the value of her taking yet another class.

She thinks she's spending too much money on decorating her apartment and buying new tech toys. She even starts to question her eating habits, wondering why she always wants to invite people over so she can cook for them. Mostly though, Melissa is worried that she's feeling stuck because she's too invested in the life she created for herself and is so secure with her connections there.

Melissa asks herself if Alex is right about her relationship with Chris. Is her uncertainty really about wanting to get married and have a family? Melissa questions why she and Chris aren't more serious. Maybe something is wrong with her, that at twenty-seven she still hasn't made a relationship work.

Although she has been through a similar dilemma before, it takes some time before Melissa realizes how much self-doubt is clouding her thinking and getting her to question practically every aspect of her life. She recalls how helpful it was to name the problem when she was struggling with her career; she decides to name the problem once again and pay close attention to what this version of self-doubt is doing to her.

Melissa starts by reading over her journal from three years ago so she can jog her memory and recall how self-doubt affected her at that time. This is so helpful that Melissa decides to make a new entry, writing down the specific ways that self-doubt is affecting her now.

Melissa creates a list: "Self-doubt is making me question my profession—and I love my writing. Self-doubt is getting me to think I'm wasting my time when I'm doing fun things with my friends—and I really do enjoy being with them and often cooking for them. Self-doubt is creating questions about my relationship with Chris, even though I know in my heart that he's really not the guy for me."

Melissa surprises herself by noticing that even as she is writing about self-doubt, she is making distinctions. This helps her see that there are many aspects of her current life she does enjoy and feel good about.

Melissa recalls leaving her parents' home in Denver ten years ago and moving to Los Angeles. She was excited; she was going to a good school; she knew what she wanted. She also remembers how difficult the transition was: There were a lot of new experiences, new people, and a new life. But she loved her courses and was highly motivated. Her life is very different now, but she wonders how she can capture that same sense of adventure and momentum to help her move forward.

Melissa titles the next entry in her journal "What's Ahead?" She knows she wants something more—a new adventure, a stimulating challenge. This doesn't necessarily mean leaving where she is but creating a different experience that will allow her to Leave the Nest while still staying connected to the people and places she cares about.

As Melissa reconnects with her past experience of competence, she decides to pay close attention to what is going on in her life right now. She surfs the Internet looking for interesting work, and one evening reads about an editorial position with a Los Angeles media company that also does business in Canada. The job description calls for someone with writing and media experience who can act as a liaison with the firm's publications in Toronto, Montreal, and Vancouver.

Melissa wonders what kind of lucky star she's living under: She loves to travel; she knows French, which might come in handy, especially in Montreal; and she already has an impressive collection of published writing. Perhaps this opportunity will allow her to keep Los Angeles as her home base but travel as part of her work. She immediately applies for the position, hoping it's a match. When Melissa calls her mother to tell her of this new possibility, her excitement is contagious. "Well done, Melissa," her mother tells her, adding, "I'm so glad for you."

WHAT CAN YOU DO?

How can you achieve independence and begin to create a life of your own without self-doubt taking over? As with all expectations, the place to start is to notice your experience on a minute-by-minute basis. The milestones for growing up inevitably lead to leaving home: Living on your own is the traditional—and expected—hallmark for independence. As a result, the pressure to Leave the Nest is so ingrained that you may find it difficult to think of it as an expectation.

The prevailing belief is that you won't learn the lessons of life until you leave home and learn those lessons on your own. As a result, you and your parents alike act as if you have to "go it alone." When things don't go well—as can happen—you begin to think something is wrong with you rather than suspect that something may be wrong with what is expected of you.

By paying attention to the importance of relationships and belonging to a community of support, you can unhook from the often isolating effects of this expectation and begin to challenge it. Lori connects to her talents and what she has learned from past experiences to help her go forward with confidence. Maria realizes she wants a continuing connection with her mother, but can still be independent at the same time. Melissa considers taking a risk and making better use of her creative ability because she knows she has a home base of security and support. Lori, Maria, and Melissa are hopeful and optimistic about their plans for the future. Their victories are not about the specific decisions they make, however, but how they overcome the self-doubt created by the pressure of this expectation.

As you once again follow the four steps, you too can triumph over self-doubt and begin to live independently but with your connections intact. Start by noticing how self-doubt and confusion are affecting you, and tell yourself that it makes sense to have those feelings now.

RECOGNIZE AND NAME THE PROBLEM

What triggers the self-doubt that comes from the pressure of this expectation? You are making every effort to do what you think you really want: You've left home, you're on your own, and you're taking another step forward. Yet, instead of jumping at the chance to show off your talents and skills as you create an independent life for yourself, you are filled with doubt. The existence of so many new possibilities and opportunities is overwhelming, and your response to them is often indecision and even paralysis.

Notice how self-doubt enters your life. For example, maybe you're looking for a job or thinking about going back to school and are considering where you want to live. Your parents would like it if you were nearby; your boyfriend wants you to move in with him; your sister asks you to come share space with her in a different city. You think it would be exciting to be on your own in a place you've never been before.

What should you do? You know you should feel fortunate to

have such a wide range of possibilities, at the same time you're overwhelmed and confused. There are too many choices and you can't get your priorities straight. You don't seem to be able to separate out what's most important to you: friends, family, a committed relationship, security, money, job happiness. You start to have dizzy spells or constant headaches. You don't eat right. You have trouble sleeping at night. You think you must be going crazy. Above all, you can't understand why this is so difficult—it's not rocket science, you just have to decide where to live.

Begin by giving a name to the problem that is grabbing hold of you. If you're at a loss about where to live, maybe the problem is "confusion" or "paralysis" or "feeling stuck." If you have to choose the next step to take in your life, perhaps the problem is "self-doubt" or "second-guessing" or "feeling wrong."

Whatever you call it, notice how the problem is affecting you and getting you to question yourself, the way you think, your past experiences, and your future goals. Nothing seems right when you are under the influence of self-doubt, especially when you have no idea where it's coming from. All you know is that you want to go forward in your life. You think Leave the Nest is something you're supposed to do—the same as everyone else.

As self-doubt takes over, you may find yourself stuck in some of the following ways:

- You are afraid to apply for a job because it's not in the "right" place.

- You think you need to start over where no one knows you.

- You don't want to discuss your situation with your parents because they might give you advice you don't like.

- You begin to hate where you live.

- You think you should marry your boyfriend, even though you're not sure he's really the one.

- You find advice from your friends to be unhelpful and off base.

- You start isolating yourself to think things through and become even more anxious and upset.

If any of these experiences seem familiar, then self-doubt is winning and you are losing. Keep in mind, however, that self-doubt should not have the upper hand; you are the one in charge of your life. By noticing how much space self-doubt is taking up in your thinking and what it's doing to you, you will be able to recognize it more readily and change your relationship to it.

You are at a time in your life when you are expected to—and also want to—make decisions about where and how to live, whether or not to become involved in a serious relationship, what career to pursue, and how to carve out your independence. These transitions are not easy, so cut yourself some slack and learn to say, "It makes sense that self-doubt would come along right now. I'm faced with lots of possibilities. I have some choices to make, and I'm not sure where they'll take me." Then try telling yourself, "Nothing is perfect, and I don't have to get it right. I just get to move forward and take the next step."

When you can say these words, you will be able to think more clearly and notice that the self-doubt you are experiencing is coming from the pressure to Leave the Nest. Then you can understand what this expectation is about and how to challenge what it's doing to you.

UNDERSTAND AND CHALLENGE THE EXPECTATION

Leave the Nest means becoming independent and creating a life of your own; it often implies having everything in place. But this expectation also means facing a future you may not have predicted and experiencing events you may not be prepared for. You don't want to be thrown like a rider on an untamed horse—you can be in charge of this expectation and can counter its power over you.

Because the pressure from this expectation can be overwhelming, it may be helpful to consider some of the specific "shoulds" you may encounter.

- You "should" finish school by a certain time.

- You "should" be on your own soon after college.

- You "should" leave your family behind and make new connections in your life.

- You "should" have a prospect for marriage before you're thirty.

- You "should" start having children before you're thirty-five.

- You "should" be able to make your own decisions without having to depend on others.

- You "should" accept the fact that you can't go home again.

As you read the above list, you can see how arbitrary these statements are. Even so, they can affect you in subtle and negative ways.

Lori thinks she "should" be on her own by now, and "should not" be still living at home. As Lori comes to understand that the self-doubt is so strong because she's in an unscripted and in-between period of her life, she realizes she can challenge the expectation and trust herself to make decisions that are right for her.

Maria wonders whether she "should" still be living with her mother now that she is married. Self-doubt arises when Maria begins to question her close relationship with her mother, making Maria worry that she may be too emotionally involved with her after all. Once Maria understands that the pressure from the expectation Leave the Nest is creating such self-doubt, she makes a distinction that she can continue to share her life with her mother and be independent at the same time.

Melissa feels stuck and thinks she "should" get on with her life. Because she's unsure what her next step should be, she starts to think she will never be fulfilled or satisfied. By recognizing the problem as self-doubt and realizing how it has affected her in the past, Melissa is able to get clear of it and see that Leave the Nest is contributing to her experience. When she decides not to give in to the expectation, she can be open to different options and opportunities.

Part of challenging the expectation Leave the Nest is for you to unmask these "shoulds," pay attention to how they influence the choices you make, and turn again to what works for you. How can you resist the "shoulds" from the expectation Leave the Nest?

- Think about how self-doubt from the pressure of this expectation is taking you away from connections that are important to you.

- Make note of the activities that you enjoy and would not want to change.

• Consider the relationships you care about and what you have learned from them.

• Notice what attracts you to certain possibilities, including friends and family, geographical location, the specifics of a new challenge or adventure.

• Recognize how your talents and skills fit with what appeals to you.

• If you think you "should" or "should not" do something, wonder what it is that you want to do instead.

By understanding how the pressure to Leave the Nest can confuse you as you move forward with your life, you can start to make distinctions and begin to get clear about what you truly value and consider important. Then you can connect to your values and beliefs as well as to those people who acknowledge and support you.

CONNECT TO WHAT YOU VALUE AND BELIEVE

The expectation Leave the Nest is such a part of our culture that you may not even be aware of how it disconnects you from yourself as well as from the people who care for and support you. Therefore, when this pressure begins to create self-doubt, it's vital that you stay close to what you hold dear: your own values, philosophy, and especially your friends and family.

Think about your response to the following questions when this expectation begins to exert pressure on you:

1. You're beginning to be bored with what you're doing and are looking for a change. What would help you decide about what you want to do next?

  a. You focus on your talents and skills.
  b. You think about where your close connections and relationships are.
  c. You wonder what part of your "old" life you want to keep connected to.
  d. You make note of who might offer support as you make a change.
  e. All of the above.

2. You begin a new endeavor in your life. What has attracted you to it?

  a. It seems familiar to you.
  b. You have special talents in this field.
  c. Someone you know suggests this might interest you.
  d. It fits your values and goals.
  e. It's a challenge you want to meet.
  f. All of the above.

3. You're deciding where you might like to live. What goes into your considerations?

  a. You have friends or family who live nearby.
  b. You've visited the area before and it seems to suit you.
  c. There's a job opportunity that's too good to pass up.
  d. Your boyfriend, husband, or partner wants to live there.
  e. All of the above.

Fortunately, there are no "right" or "wrong" answers here. Once you separate from self-doubt, any answer you give will help you focus on what you consider meaningful in your life because you will be making choices that "fit" for you. Ask yourself what your answers tell you about how you value relationships, the areas you feel most competent, and where you can best use your unique talents and skills. You will find that overcoming self-doubt and challenging this expectation include both a connection to yourself and to what you know and believe as well as a connection to persons you care about and value.

SEEK ALLIES AGAINST SELF-DOUBT

When you're struggling to become independent, you may shy away from counting too much on friends and family. If you end up sharing an apartment with your best friend from college or moving in with your boyfriend right away or even returning home for a few months while you wait for a job possibility to materialize, you may think you are taking the easy way out. How can you possibly have allies in these circumstances?

Allies are people you turn to who can hold your hand in your distress and witness your success; if you're afraid to ask for help because you think you're too attached to them, you've lost your community of support when you need it the most.

Remember that taking steps toward independence doesn't mean leaving behind those who love you. In fact, making important decisions are easier when they come from within a context of love and care as well as a community where you belong.

As you move forward in creating a life of your own, your mother can be your strongest ally because she genuinely wants the best for you. She is also affected by the pressure for you to Leave the Nest, however, and may think that she should leave you alone. As Maria learns, there are specific ways you can keep your important connection to your mother and be truly independent at the same time.

Helping your mother. For many mothers, one of the most difficult times is when you leave home. Think about what it will be like when you have children: You will spend years of your life caring for them and will always want to protect them. You will want to stay close to them, as your mother wants to remain close to you. When your children eventually go off on their own, you will wish them the best but also experience an unimaginable loss when they disconnect from you as Leave the Nest dictates.

There are times, however, when your mother may not be available to you because of her own life circumstances, and you may not believe that you can reconnect to her. Consider what you and your mother can share together realistically, and let her know that you value her interest and concern. If your mother can be present in your life, she will most likely welcome the opportunity to support you as you seek independence. Think about what experiences you can share with her as you prepare to leave home, graduate from college, move to a new city, become engaged, decide on a new job, travel abroad, or enter graduate school.

- Let your mother know your thoughts on what new ventures you are considering.

- Discuss with her the pros and cons about a course of action you want to take.

- Tell her what is influencing your decision to move to a certain city, take a specific job, attend a particular school, consider marriage.

• Keep her posted about your progress as you search for something new and different.

• Assume that she wants to help, so let her know what would be helpful: a simple acknowledgment of your situation, giving you ideas as you think through a problem, reminding you of your past accomplishments, congratulating you on a job well done.

Your mother doesn't want to contribute to any self-doubt you might be experiencing from Leave the Nest, so you might remember that she is by your side, which is much different from you being too emotionally attached to her.

Don't forget to include your mentors as allies in your evolving independence and call upon their wisdom. Pick and choose who among them may be the best able to understand what you are going through as different situations and challenges arise along the way.

Helping your women friends. Your peer group is undoubtedly facing a similar form of self-doubt, so you may have become estranged from each other as the expectation Leave the Nest creates pressure on all of you. Once you relax about your ability to remain connected to those who care about you, you will be able to count on some of your women friends as allies. These may include women who have known you over a period of time and have seen you struggle with other expectations that they too have wrestled with.

• Talk to your friends about their experience of moving toward an independent life. Share stories about what works and what doesn't.

• Let your allies know how you are challenging the expectation Leave the Nest, including the tactics you find most useful.

• Tell them about your reflecting on past moments of competence and confidence, which help you know it's possible to make a life of your own.

• Keep your allies up to date about your progress so they can support you on a regular basis.

• Celebrate both small and large victories with them—especially when you are in a transition period—to remind yourself that life is a process and new opportunities open up all the time.

The expectation Leave the Nest can subtly eat away at you and get you to doubt your connection to your friends, so it is important that you continue to think of your friends as allies, who will stay by your side.

Helping the men in your life. Men as well as women are affected by this expectation, so the men in your life will not be surprised when they hear how self-doubt is interfering with your progress toward creating your own life. Because you so highly value connections, you know that staying close to people who support you will help you to leave the nest in a way that works for you. Share that knowledge with the men who care about you.

• Tell them how important it is for you to have them by your side as you move toward an independent life.

• Share what you have learned about living on your own and what values help you make decisions about how to go forward.

• Make plans to spend time together so you can let them know what you are going through. Ask them how they deal with similar transitions in their own lives.

Stay in tune with the possibilities that all your allies offer you to learn, share, grow, ask for help, and celebrate success. Those who love you will want you be free of fear and self-doubt as you become an independent woman with a life of your own.

GOING FORWARD WITH COMPETENCE

The expectation Leave the Nest has particular potency at this time in your life because it encompasses so many major transitions and changes, including leaving home, graduating from college, deciding where to live, finding a job, creating your own home, planning your future with another person, and continuing to make decisions about what to do next. When you can redefine what it is you are experiencing and determine what's best for you in your individual circumstances, you will be well on your way to living independently.

CHAPTER SEVEN

Follow the Rules

EVERYTHING FINALLY SEEMS to be working out for Sylvia. She's enjoying the Washington, D.C., scene; the congresswoman has moved her into a more responsible position; she works out every morning with friends from the office; and, best of all, her fiancé, Seth, having finished his doctoral degree in Berkeley, is moving to Virginia to look for work so he can be near her. Sylvia has put to rest the doubts from the expectation "Be Popular" and is ready for whatever life offers next.

To mark what feels like a more settled existence, Sylvia decides to take up the violin again for the first time since college. After a few lessons to smooth out the rough edges, she's surprised to discover how passionate she still feels about playing. Sylvia connects to her love for music in a different way than she ever has to law, and begins to ask herself if she should change careers.

"Maybe I'm going in the wrong direction," she says. "I went to law school because I knew I would be good at it and could make a living. But now I don't know what I want. I'm caught in the middle between law and music, both of which I like. I wonder if I was thoughtful enough when I was making plans for the future or just based my decisions on what I was supposed to do."

The expectation "Follow the Rules" requires that you go along a clearly marked path toward a well-defined goal. There are certain steps you think you're supposed to take that will assure you of success, such as forming a significant relationship, embarking on a career, establishing financial independence, maintaining your appearance, making friends, and choosing where you want to live. Like Sylvia, however, you may find yourself unprepared for the self-doubt that can appear as you encounter unpredictable events along the way.

There are always surprise bumps in the road, and some can send you into self-doubt instead of allowing you to reflect on and reassess what is happening to you. You may find yourself questioning the direction you've chosen and wonder if you've taken the right road after all. By challenging the expectation Follow the Rules, you will be able to reflect on past decisions, continuing with those choices that fit for you and considering what changes you want to make.

THE DILEMMA

There are times when things fall apart and other times when things come together. Our lives are cyclical, and we can all too easily become caught in one part of a cycle or the other. When the unexpected happens, as it most inevitably will, you may think your life is falling apart; you may even fear that, like Humpty Dumpty, you'll never be able to put your life back together again.

Does it ever happen that you think your life is moving along smoothly when suddenly one aspect goes haywire? You may have just received a promotion at work, then find out that your boyfriend is being transferred; you may move to another city only to discover that the job you were so sure about is no longer available; you may suffer a physical injury and be unable to exercise for several months; or you may be financially self-sufficient but feel lost in your social life.

Other times nothing feels right. You may accomplish a longed-for goal and instead of being happy, wonder what's wrong with you that this didn't happen sooner. Life is full of expectations, and Follow the Rules tells you that you should want to succeed at each of them. Tired of juggling all these balls, you find yourself reacting to this pressure by going on automatic and making important decisions without the necessary reflection to consider what you really do want.

Self-doubt prevents you from connecting to your intuition, unlike self-reflection, which allows you to question and take action because it comes from listening to yourself. When you overcome the self-doubt created by the expectation Follow the Rules, you will be able to reflect on past decisions, learn from the roads you take and those you don't, and create rules that work for you.

Sylvia is reconnecting with a past passion for the violin that leads her to question and doubt her decision to pursue her current career in law and government. Amy, who you met as she struggled with the expectation "Have a Career," is experiencing success as director of marketing and sales for a large corporation in Boston until constant exhaustion threatens to disrupt both her professional and personal life. She begins to doubt her life direction and wonder if she's made bad decisions along the way. Colleen, who succeeded in overcoming self-doubt from the expectation "Make It on Your Own," is still living in Seattle near her family and friends; when her new fiancé, Simon, tells her that he wants to relocate to Houston, Colleen becomes fearful and anxious because she thinks she has to join him there and leave all the people she cares about behind.

SELF-REFLECTION

At twenty-nine, Sylvia believes her life is in order: She has a meaningful career, financial stability, a place she calls home, a potential life partner, and a support network she can count on. She has "followed the rules" and made a solid beginning for a rich and fulfilling future.

Sylvia's renewed enthusiasm for the violin, however, is making her wonder if she has taken the wrong turn somewhere along the road. Her life seems to lack personal meaning—something unique and special just for her—and she's not at all sure her career in law can continue to fulfill her. Sylvia's needs have changed, and what used to be important to her no longer carries the same weight. Sylvia finds herself wondering if her past decisions were based on what she really wanted or because she was supposed to follow a prescribed path.

Sylvia thinks back to her passion for the violin. Her parents encouraged her to take lessons from the time she was very young, and Sylvia continued to perform from elementary school through college. She knew she was talented and loved the sense of accomplishment that her playing gave her. She gave up the violin in law school, but now with her career well on its way, she is delighted to rediscover her special gift for playing beautiful music.

Sylvia decides to audition for a local symphony orchestra, and is thrilled when she is asked to join. Now Sylvia spends practically all of her spare time practicing or performing with the orchestra. She realizes that she has embarked on an important new venture in her life, but begins to worry how she'll be able to manage her time after she and Seth start living together and want to do things as a couple. Sylvia is happier than she can remember, but thoughts of giving up her law career to play the violin full time start swirling in her head and she's concerned.

"What will people think?" she wonders. "My parents have always told me that my music should be something I do for my own entertainment, not a life commitment. Also, I'm not sure that changing careers at this point is such a smart move because it will be much more difficult to support myself as a violinist."

Self-doubt sets in, and Sylvia starts to question her desires. "What do I really want?" she keeps asking herself. "Did I decide on a career too soon? I thought I wanted to be a lawyer and work for the government, but now I'm not so sure. I've done all the right things—why should all these thoughts be popping up now?"

The questioning is incessant. "Is the chance to play my violin with the symphony a sign that I should make a change?" she wonders. "And what will Seth say? How will he view my switching gears, not to mention that he might have to support us indefinitely? I have no idea what to do."

Sylvia has lost her balance. She is caught by a conflict of desires, complicated by the fact that she has successfully fulfilled all the expectations asked of her but is unsure if they really reflect her goals and desires.

Sylvia knows that her mother is proud of her accomplishments, and decides to have a conversation with her about her dilemma. Her mother listens carefully, then says, "Sylvia, when you first moved to Washington and were struggling with your social life, you told me that it helped to name the problem. What about trying the same thing again?"

Sylvia can't believe her ears. Her mother is talking about the self-doubt, not about what specific career Sylvia should pursue. The acknowledgment that self-doubt is what Sylvia needs to be paying attention to is both helpful and reassuring.

"You're right, Mom," she says. "I'm caught in the middle between two things I love—continuing my career in government or devoting myself to my music. I would call the problem 'questioning' and 'doubt' because it's making me wonder if I had my priorities straight when I was younger. But I know I won't be able to think clearly about any of this until I get rid of the doubt."

Once Sylvia names the problem with the help of her mother, she begins to see how overpowering the problem has become; she is questioning her past choices and present course of action. Sylvia knows she wants to free herself from this confusion or else it will be too difficult to distinguish second-guessing from real self-reflection.

Ever since she can remember, Sylvia has felt pressure to have everything work smoothly and be in place. She has tried to hold on to what she thinks will be good for her, to what she really wants, but now she realizes she doesn't know what that is. Sylvia wonders if she made her decisions based on what she thought was expected of her; although she knows her choices weren't necessarily wrong, they just don't seem carefully thought out and considered.

Sylvia realizes she needs to make a clean break from self-doubt to help her think back on the different choices she has made in her life. This realization helps her to reconnect to her intuition, and she begins to recognize that many of her decisions were good ones after all. Sylvia knows she will now give more consideration to her future decisions and be especially attuned to any messages that tell her to Follow the Rules.

Sylvia still has a huge decision to make. She talks more with her mother, she decides to invite her friends over for dinner to share what she is thinking, and she organizes a weekend away with Seth so they can discuss their future together, including decisions about her career. Sylvia knows she has options as well as friends and family who are her allies. She can take the next step in her life, whatever it may be, with clarity and confidence.

WHY ME?

When we left Amy in the chapter "Have a Career," she was running the marketing division of a high-tech firm in Boston. Over the last year, she has successfully settled into a job that suits her; she also has weathered all the layoffs in her industry and is assured that both she and her company are secure—at least for the time being.

At twenty-eight, Amy is delighted with her life, especially since she met Ben, a writer for a national business magazine. They enjoy hanging out together, plus Ben is attentive and respectful in a way that Amy really likes. They've been going together for six months, and both of them know it's serious.

Recently, however, Amy finds that she is tired all the time. She's having a hard time concentrating at work and finds herself becoming irritable when she's out with Ben and other friends. Even though Amy is totally exhausted, she's having trouble sleeping at night and often finds it difficult to keep alert during the day.

Amy is becoming worried about the possible ramifications of her situation. When she was a teenager, she had trouble with constant headaches, which were eventually diagnosed as stress related. Now, Amy is worried that stress may again be the problem.

"Maybe it's all in my head," Amy says. "I just can't imagine what could be creating such tension and pressure in my life. I've done everything right—or so I thought. Why is this happening to me?"

When I ask Amy what she means by "doing everything right," she says she is moving along on the path she was supposed to follow. She went to a prestigious school so she could get a good job in the business world, then moved to a big city where there would be more career opportunities. She has been steadily promoted at work, and created a home and social life of her own. Now, best of all, she has a marriage possibility.

"It doesn't make sense to be this tired all the time," she says. "I don't have any more stress in my life than usual. I'm not a bad person, I just can't figure out what's going on."

I wonder how Amy makes a connection between being

exhausted, which could be the result of a variety of reasons, and the decisions she has made in her life.

"I don't know why I feel this way," she responds. "It almost seems like a punishment for something I've done wrong. Before, my life just fell into place. Even though I followed the rules, I'm doing what I want. Now everything is up in the air and I don't know what's going on."

Amy and I talk about how being tired is a genuine experience. I mention that it may be important for her to check out what medical conditions may be contributing to her constant exhaustion, and perhaps she could make an appointment with her doctor for a thorough checkup. We then discuss how the exhaustion is affecting her emotionally as well as physically. I suggest that it may be important to address the fear as well as her real experience of tiredness.

"I can't stop blaming myself for feeling so incapacitated," she begins. "Now I find fault in everything I do. I'm in a lose-lose situation, and can't seem to find my way out of it."

I remind Amy how naming the problem and seeing how it affected her had helped when she struggled with the expectation "Have a Career." What would she name the problem now?

Amy reflects for a moment, then says, "Before it was 'lack of confidence,' but now it's more like 'self-criticism,' " she says. "I'm constantly trying to figure out what I've done wrong to make this happen. All I do is obsess about how exhausted I am and end up overanalyzing every detail about how I feel."

Amy realizes that she's been complaining a lot, and fears that Ben may leave her because she's been so difficult to be with lately. She's also concerned that she may have to change jobs because she just doesn't seem to have enough energy to do her work.

Mostly she thinks about how she must have "gotten it wrong" to have this happen when everything was going so well in her life. But Amy doesn't know what that "wrong" turn or bad decision might be.

As Amy describes what self-criticism is doing to her, she realizes the problem is not that she's done something wrong or even that she's constantly worn out. In fact, she has only done what she thinks is the "right" thing to do. Amy realizes the only way she can overcome the self-criticism is to pay attention to what is working for her at this point in her life.

Amy knows she needs support as she tackles what seems like a very big problem. The first thing she does is call her friend Taisha, who she knows will talk straight to her. "You've got to stop fooling around and start managing your life," Taisha tells her. "Instead of worrying about what's making you so tired, you have to begin to deal with it."

Amy knows Taisha is right, and the two of them draw up a list of what Amy needs to do. To begin, Amy may need to change some of the physical aspects of her job, so she decides to make an appointment to speak with her supervisor at work. Next, she has to check with her doctors to see if there are specific exercises or diet or physical therapy that will help her have more energy; she will also request referrals to a stress-reduction clinic and a yoga class. Finally, Amy decides to ask Ben for his support rather than continue to block him out. Together they make adjustments to their time, so that they can create activities they both enjoy and where Amy won't get so easily worn out.

Amy's talk with Taisha convinces her that she can't allow self-criticism to continue to make her overanalyze why she is so tired or blame herself for the decisions she's made in her life.

Although Amy may have "followed the rules," she knows her choices have taken her to a good place.

"I knew I could count on you to be honest with me," Amy says, thanking Taisha. "Now I can keep going forward, try to deal with whatever life throws at me, and not be so hard on myself."

WHAT RULES?

The pressure from the expectation "Make It on Your Own" is finally easing for Colleen. She is making enough money at her software company in Seattle to feel financially secure for the first time in her life, and at twenty-five, feels happy and successful. Colleen lives near her family, who she visits frequently; has a close group of friends; continues to be promoted at work; and recently became engaged to Simon, a medical student who she met in her rowing group.

A nagging problem, however, has just raised its head. Simon was recently accepted into a pediatrics residency program at a hospital in Houston, and Colleen has no desire to leave her family, friends, and job in Seattle. "Why can't Simon just stay here?" she asks. "There are great hospitals in Seattle. Besides, his parents also live nearby and they would love us to stay close."

Colleen is concerned that Simon has already reached a decision on his own. She is also afraid he would resent her if she were to ask him to stay in Seattle, and finds herself wondering who wrote the rules that she's the one who is supposed to follow. Colleen is also struggling with how to think about what to do, let alone how to begin to take action.

Up to now, Colleen has been on the path she assumes will lead to a full and satisfying life. She studied hard in high school in order to be accepted into the state university, and while she lived at home for a while, she worked overtime to establish an independent life for herself. She entered a profession she likes and that pays well, and her company recognizes her talents and rewards her for them. Not only that, Seattle is where she grew up and has her roots. Why should she leave all this behind?

Anxiety begins to set in. Colleen thinks there must be something wrong with her that she can't take this next logical step in her life. She's done everything else that was marked out for her. Why is she starting to question the rules now?

Colleen wants to talk with Simon about her reservations about moving to Houston with him, but she is afraid of his reaction. She imagines that he already assumes it's a done deal—the hospital will help them find housing; she'll get a job; they will make new friends and create a home together. Simon is continually pointing out that Houston is a relatively short flight from Seattle, and they can easily come home for holidays. He thinks it's easy.

But Colleen knows she needs to talk to someone. Although she usually goes to her father for advice, this time she wants to discuss her situation with her mother. When Colleen calls to make a date for dinner, her mother seems pleased but surprised. It's unusual for just the two of them to get together, but her mother is genuinely interested and sympathetic to Colleen's story.

"The world is so different from when I was your age," her mother tells her. "Getting married used to mean automatically following your husband, no questions asked. Today you have so many more choices. You can Have a Career, a chance to live on your own, a separate social life from your husband. Maybe all these options make it more difficult."

"I know, Mom," Colleen says. "But what should I do?"

Her mother pauses to collect her thoughts. "It seems that the problem may be the fear and anxiety you're feeling," she says. "This reminds me when you first started working after college and were trying so hard to make ends meet. I know your father and I couldn't help you out financially as much as we would have liked and that you were very afraid. But I saw you turn it around and make a good life for yourself. How did you do it?"

Colleen remembers back to only a couple of years ago. Yes, she was scared and anxious from the pressure to make it on her own. The fear feels the same now, only this time it's about a very different issue.

"Thanks, Mom," Colleen says. "It's fear, or self-doubt, that is getting me stuck. I feel caught thinking I 'should' follow a certain rule, but I don't know which rule it is that I'm supposed to follow: Be independent? Stay close to the people I care about? Follow Simon and make a home where he goes? If I can get rid of the fear, I can think more clearly."

"Maybe it's not an 'either-or' situation," Colleen's mother says. "Maybe it's a 'both-and.'"

Colleen laughs as she remembers her mother telling her this while she was growing up. She knows she made the right decision to come to her mother for advice. Despite how helpful it has been, Colleen still wonders how all her choices will eventually work together. Their conversation has helped her see that the problem isn't the dilemma she's facing but the fear that prevents her from sorting it out. Colleen also understands that the fear is what is keeping her stuck. It's stopping her from getting information about what life may be like in Houston, and worse, it's inhibiting her from approaching Simon—they haven't explored what it would mean for him to stay in Seattle. Colleen knows her next step is to talk to Simon about a possible compromise that would work for both of them.

Colleen realizes that her life doesn't have to be a series of well-marked steps. Her past choices have been on a more-traveled path, but she now knows there are always alternative routes that can also take her where she wants to go. Once fear is out of the way, Colleen can choose to follow rules of her own making.

WHAT CAN YOU DO?

The problem with expectations is that they slip into your life in such a way that they make you think they belong to you. From the time you are young, you are told what you need to do in order to be successful. The pressure to fulfill these expectations continues to build up over the years until, once you're in your twenties and out on your own, you begin to feel like you have to keep going forward or somehow the world will come crashing in on you.

So you keep on keepin' on. Sometimes you get one thing in place, like a good job, and something else falls apart or isn't quite right. Or you have two or three things taken care of, but you just can't seem to find the right relationship. Then maybe just when you think you have it all together, a single unexpected event or circumstance occurs—you lose your job, your boyfriend bails, a member of your family becomes seriously ill—and you're sure your entire life is going to disintegrate. Like Sylvia, you may begin to question your professional choices; or like Amy, you start to experience unexpected health problems; or like Colleen, you are unsure what "rule" to follow as you try to maintain your independence and commit to a relationship at the same time.

Life is not predictable. It's full of surprises, some of which are exciting and pleasing, others that are challenging and open the door to self-reflection—or perhaps self-doubt. Unfortunately, the expectation Follow the Rules doesn't allow for variations or for the unexpected. The path is straight and narrow, and self-doubt can easily find a way into your experience when there is even the slightest deviation in your plans.

When self-doubt enters your life, you start to question and second-guess your choices. You wonder what has happened that you didn't get it right, and you think you're a failure. Even the decisions you made in the past that seem to be working are suddenly suspect. Something is wrong with your job. You don't like where you live. You realize that you've never been happy with the way you look. You're afraid you have to take a cut in pay and won't be able to afford your apartment. Your friends aren't supportive. Your boyfriend is distant. Nothing works, and the smallest setback makes you think your whole life is a mess.

In the best of all possible worlds, it would be great to be able to use unpredictable events as an opportunity to reflect on your decisions. This would allow your life to be richer, more complex, and, in the long run, more satisfying. But when self-doubt makes its appearance, you become blind to this possibility. You feel bad, and think you must have made a terrible mistake or a wrong turn somewhere along the way.

As with all the expectations, start by paying attention to what is happening to you on a daily basis. Remember that in this expectation, self-doubt can be sparked by any occurrence that is not in line with the path you are already on. Whatever the trigger may be, the problem is what it's doing to you, how it's getting you to mistrust your own intuition and drain you of confidence.

RECOGNIZE AND NAME THE PROBLEM

When you are blindsided by the unpredictable, self-doubt—or some version of it—can materialize in an instant. Your initial reaction is to try to figure out why this is happening to you and make sense of what's going on. Instead of trying to understand *why* an unexpected event is throwing you off course, concentrate instead on *how* it's affecting you. Pay attention to what your experience is. Are you agitated, worried, anxious, sad, overly concerned, uncertain? As you know from the past, identifying and naming the problem will help you become clear of it. Once you take a half step back and notice how the problem is affecting you, you are already reducing its power over you.

By sharing her dilemma about her career with her mother, Sylvia recognizes that the problem is "questioning" and "doubt," which is clouding her thinking and making her feel confused. Amy believes the problem is her low energy, which is very real, but notices that along with the tiredness comes a great deal of "self-criticism." Colleen realizes that the problem is not whether or not she should follow Simon but the "fear" and "anxiety" that surround this important decision.

How are you experiencing the pressure to Follow the Rules? You may be living your life in ways you think you should and then, out of the blue, something goes awry. Because this unexpected turn of events doesn't fit your plan, you find yourself unprepared and without a road map to follow. While you try to sidestep what's going on and keep moving forward, the dilemma soon is taking up more and more of your time.

Keep in mind that the problem is not about how to resolve the situation but about how you are being influenced by what is happening. Once you notice the specific effects, you can start to name the problem. Consider if any of the following responses sound familiar.

- You're confused, worried, and can't understand what is going on.

- You are wondering if you did something wrong and what it could be; you think you're a failure.

- You retrace your steps, trying to figure out what you could have done differently.

- You believe you're being punished or cursed.

- You forget what you used to know and close yourself off to new information.

Soon you are obsessively going over all your decisions, second-guessing each and every one of them. You may be irritable with your friends and family, your job may be suffering, your quiet time no longer seems so quiet, you can't figure out how to relax, or you feel stressed out and overcome with doubt.

Now you can begin to name the problem, making sure that it captures your experience of how you did—or didn't—Follow the Rules. Whether you call what's going on self-doubt, second-guessing, self-criticism, confusion, fear, or anxiety, notice the extent of its influence over you and decide it has no place in your life.

UNDERSTAND AND CHALLENGE THE EXPECTATION

Follow the Rules probably doesn't sound like an expectation you think you must meet. Most likely, you were brought up to have your own mind and be your own unique person. So how is it that you now find yourself trapped by this expectation and are experiencing such pressure from it?

You have been on a course where the road signs are clearly marked: college, career, independence, marriage. If you stray too far from the path, there are subtle but important corrections to get you back on track. The pressure is hardly noticeable because everyone else is doing the same thing—or so you believe. If for some reason you take an alternative route or stray off course, you may wonder if something is wrong with you.

So you go along "following the rules"—not realizing that's what you are doing—when suddenly, or so it seems, something unexpected trips you up and self-doubt sets in. Only by working to clear away the feeling of insecurity will you become aware that it comes from this expectation and be ready to challenge it.

Bringing the expectation into the open and exposing it is the key to making careful and thoughtful decisions about the path you wish to take in your life. Now you can begin to ask yourself:

- Why did I take a certain course of study in college?

- What was behind my decision to pursue the career I followed?

- What influences the way I spend money?

- What are my reasons for the choices I make in clothes, food, exercise?

- How did I happen to choose the friends who enrich my social life?

- What attracted me to the place where I live?

- Why am I interested in my present relationship and do I want to commit permanently to it?

Think about your responses to these questions. Use the dreams and visions you hold for your future as your guide, and acknowledge that the decisions you have made in the past reflected your best judgment at the time. Reconsider your choices and wonder if there are any adjustments you would like to make now. Realize that life is a process, and even what you may consider "wrong" decisions have led you to a place where you can continue to learn and grow.

CONNECT TO WHAT YOU VALUE AND BELIEVE

Ask yourself what you want. Connecting to what you value and believe means paying attention to and carefully crafting what you want. It may very well be that the choices you've made up until now are close approximations to what you desire, and your current path suits you fine. On the other hand, you may find yourself questioning the direction your life is taking. As you separate from self-doubt and challenge the expectation Follow the Rules, you can consider previous decisions you want to honor and others you want to change.

Self-reflection is an acquired wisdom. As you begin to examine your life choices without judgment or justification, you may come to understand that your past decisions were made with your best intentions and with the information you had available at the time. Notice when the following occurs:

- You followed the well-traveled path and were rewarded and recognized for doing so.

- You were encouraged to follow your own path.

- You made decisions "outside the lines" and there were corrections, or your choices were acknowledged and valued.

- You bravely went forward, not sure about your decisions but willing to take a risk.

- Your choices felt like mistakes, but you learned from your experience.

- No matter what you did, someone was there to support you.

Sometimes the answers are not so apparent. Try to think what you find most pleasing about your life now and the choices you made to get there. Trace the history of those decisions, and recall the past events that led to where you are today. Give yourself credit for how you've created your own path and followed your own rules.

As you reflect on your current situation, think about the people in your past who supported your desires and wishes as well as the experiences that fit how you want to live your life now:

- Do your parents have an interest or background in the career you are pursuing?

- Is your choice of geographical location rich with memories of good experiences or close friends who also live there?

- Are you able to create relationships wherever you go that allow you to be flexible about where to live?

• Do you have a special desire to go to a different country, follow a certain passion (music, art, theater, cooking), or explore a new possibility?

• Do you have a parent, grandparent, aunt, uncle, cousin, former teacher, godparent, or friend who has seen your talents and skills and would encourage you to pursue something different that would fulfill you?

As you come to live a life that is more of your own making, you will remember past events that confirm your current choices and recall details from your history that fit with where you are now. The fabric of your life will become richer and more complex as you continue to fill it with people from both your past and present to walk along the road with you.

SEEK ALLIES AGAINST SELF-DOUBT

As you go forward in your life, making new decisions and perhaps even changing your chosen path, your friends or family may not be caught up with some of the subtle differences in your thinking or the way you are redirecting your course. Don't assume that the people who you care about will automatically know or accept what you are doing, especially if they think of you in a certain way and couldn't possibly know what has intervened in your life between then and now.

By learning to go easy on yourself, you can also find ways to be more patient with your friends and family. It's safe to assume they want the best for you, so help them show their concern in ways that please you.

Helping your mother. Your mother has been with you from the time you took your first step and had no inkling what the future would hold. She has seen you through all the important stages in your growing up, watching you struggle with each expectation you encounter and wrestle with the difficult "what-shall-I-do-with-my-life" decisions. Your mother knows you have your own hopes and dreams, and, in the best of times, she wants to support you in fulfilling them. If, perhaps, your mother is struggling with her own life problems, consider how you would want her to be available to you and try to think of her with gentle respect.

Think about your growing-up experience and what your mother has shared with you:

- Do you have a photograph of your mother holding you as a baby, and does it help remind you that she cares for you?

- Did you ever talk to her about school, friends, teachers, plays, projects?

- Do you remember what you didn't tell her and wish you had or were glad you didn't?

- When you first went away from home (college, moving out, or travel), what did you share about your experience?

- Are you getting better at being clear about what you need and want from her so she can thoughtfully give you the kind of backup you would like?

Share the knowledge you are gaining from your current self-reflection with your mother, and include her in your thinking as you wonder what decisions to make next. Tell her about the life lessons you have already learned.

You and your mother may have a unique history of connection with each other. For example, when Sylvia is filled with questioning and doubt, she knows she can turn to her mother for help because of other times in the past when she trusted her mother's judgment and insights. Colleen also sees that her mother is an appropriate ally when she helps Colleen reconnect with her victory over fear and anxiety during her struggle with "Have a Career."

Share some of your growing-up experiences with your mother and see how they relate to your present situation. Your mother will welcome the chance to be included in your life, as you both will benefit from keeping your relationship a close and supportive one.

Helping your women friends. Being with friends who care about you during this uncertain time is critical. When you look back on your twenties, you may consider these friendships among your most important memories.

As you now face and challenge the most complex of all expectations, Follow the Rules, you can share what you are going through with the women who are by your side and have been there through your past struggles and victories. Although some friends will delight in your accomplishments, others will disappoint and be seemingly unresponsive. They may have difficulties in their own lives that can get in the way of their appreciating what is going on for you and understanding what you consider important.

If you expect your friends to share in your joy, it's helpful to tell them what you would like to hear from them. You might start by saying, "I want you to be excited that I'm doing this," or "This means a great deal to me, so I want you to be happy for me."

No one knows what you are going through as well as you. Tell your friends what is happening in your life in such a way that they can truly see what is important to you. Don't forget to let them know how much you value their support. Amy knows to go to her friend Taisha because she will "talk straight" to her. This allows Amy to eventually work out a plan with her boyfriend, Ben.

Think about how to keep your friends on board as your allies:

• Use all the modern means of communication at your fingertips (instant messaging, cell phone, e-mail) to keep them posted on what is happening in your life—especially if you are facing a big decision or a new challenge.

• Share your disappointments in the context of your successes so your friends can acknowledge your concerns as well as celebrate your progress.

• Create real, live celebrations when you can. Bring your friends together to eat, drink, and toast your accomplishments.

• Make distinctions for your friends about what decisions you have made that either advanced or frustrated your progress. Share what you have learned with them.

• Laugh a lot about how you thought things would turn out one way and ended up turning out another.

• Share your similarities and differences, and delight in your uniqueness.

As you leave your twenties and form committed relation-ships or start your own family, continue to treasure and nur-ture your friendships, as they can truly stay with you forever. As your parents pass on and your life changes, your friends will be your mainstay of support. Never underestimate their impor-tance.

Helping the men in your life. Fathers, husbands, and other men in your life often feel compelled to do the right thing; if for some reason they think they fall short, they are overcome with feelings of inadequacy. Because of this, they could easily assume your experience is similar. As a result, you may appreciate their well-meaning advice and intentions but not always find that their suggestions fit your situation.

Helping your father to be your ally often means letting him know you are aware he wants to be supportive, but his sugges-tions may not be what you are looking for. You want him to try to understand and appreciate your experience, and tell you that he is on your side. Even though you are certain your father cares for you, you want to hear him say it.

What memories of your relationship with your father will help you know when you can turn to him for support and invite him to be an ally?

• Can you remember him holding your hand as you learned to walk?

• Did you ever talk to him about boys and sports or your goals and dreams?

• Did you let him know when you were disappointed, hurt, or saddened, and ask him to just be with you?

- Did you sometimes hang out and do what he wanted, just because you liked being with him?

- Do you know that even though your father may give you unwanted advice, he wants the best for you?

As you go forward and make decisions that shape the course of your life, continue to turn to both your parents for all the support they can give you. The other important men in your life—from husbands to brothers to friends—are also often pressured by a need to get it right. They do want to be helpful, so accept their sincerity and appreciate that they are acting with your best interests at heart. Love them for what they offer you. Remember, having allies is priceless.

GOING FORWARD WITH COMPETENCE

Your twenties are a decade of decisions. When an unexpected turn of events occurs, it can throw your life into disarray and get you to question the path you have taken. The problem is not what decisions to change or new directions to follow, but to understand how you are caught by the pressure of the expectation to Follow the Rules. Once you expose the self-doubt this expectation creates and turn it into self-reflection, you can confirm old decisions, make new ones, and face your future with confidence.

I hope you can more clearly see that you do not have to follow the specifics of any expectation that affects you. You can pick what fits for you and then choose what you want to do. Most important, you can craft your own life in a manner that suits you. When self-doubt hangs in the way, it can throw you off track—whether it's your track or one society has created for you. Your task is to get clear of the self-doubt so you can cut and paste your life to fit your desires.

How do you know what you want? Keep asking yourself that question. There is no definitive answer; however, you can continue to reinvent yourself in true twenty-first-century fashion and see that life offers many different paths filled with wonderful adventures and possibilities.

From Doubt to Understanding

IN THE MID- TO late 1990s I first began to notice how many of the young women I was working with were dealing with anxiety, fear, and self-doubt. Among the women from whom I learned at that time was my twentysomething goddaughter, who was finishing college, studying anthropology, and sharing with me her experience of anxiety. She and I talked frequently about why the young women I knew, including her, were experiencing such distress. This book is my response to the many conversations and learning—both from my goddaughter and from all the young women I have worked with over the past many years as well.

As you know, many changes have occurred in the world since the turn of the millennium. Terrorist attacks, invasions, scares from biochemical threats, and worldwide diseases, not to mention an ailing economy, have assailed the world at large. Who wouldn't experience some form of anxiety? Yet, while we must deal with such uncertainty, we also benefit from increased technological advances as well as new creations in art, music, and literature. We continue to try to advance the opportunities for the human race on a global level. We recognize that we don't exist in a vacuum, but are influenced by the context of our surroundings.

Young women are living in a time of great opportunity. Despite periods of economic downturn, the opportunity I am talking about is relative to what women experienced when I was in my twenties, when your mothers and grandmothers were in their twenties, and when women had to fight for the chance to do anything other than leave their growing-up home and move to their husband's home. Not that doing this was such a terrible option—it was just that it was pretty much the only one.

Feminism offered women an entire new range of possibilities, which may now feel to you more like expectations and demands. The pressure to make your life work combined with the anxiety of living in a world filled with unexpected events is a powerful mix. This is why it is so crucial for you to focus on overcoming self-doubt and defining your life on your own terms so you can claim the power and control that you may not even realize you have.

Many young women tell me that they are always amazed how things work out when they follow their intuition. They say their lives come together almost magically; it "just happens" like a lightbulb suddenly going on or a lightning bolt flashing in the sky. But I believe that change occurs as an almost imperceptible movement over time: The many small things you do take you in a certain direction and prepare you for what then seems like a sudden shift.

Following the four steps to overcoming self-doubt will help you create change in your life. Like the four seasons, you will return to them over and over as you challenge each of the seven expectations. Remember, however, that self-doubt can reemerge when you least expect it, so be prepared to recognize it, name it, and decide, once again, that you want nothing of it. Then you can begin to challenge the expectation that is creating such pressure for you. By keeping connected to what you value and believe and relying on allies to provide you with love and support, you will be better able to take risks and meet new challenges along the way.

I often ask my clients what is the one thing they would take away from our conversations together. From the larger conversation of this book, I would hope that you come to see that by vanquishing self-doubt, you can trust your intuition, hold on to your own wisdom, know you belong to a larger community, and make the decisions you want with both confidence and conviction.

RESOURCES

The following list includes books, Web sites, and suggestions from other young women that you may find helpful as you make decisions about your life—in your own time and on your own terms.

BOOKS

Bengis, Ingrid. *Combat in the Erogenous Zone*. New York: Harper-Perennial, 1991.

Chödrön, Pema. *When Things Fall Apart: Heart Advice for Difficult Times*. Boston: Shambhala, 1997.

Coehlo, Paulo. *The Valkyries*. San Francisco: HarperSanFrancisco, 1995.

Faludi, Susan. *Backlash: The Undeclared War Against American Women*. New York: Crown, 1991.

Friedan, Betty. *The Feminine Mystique*. New York: Norton, 1963.

Friedan, Betty. *The Second Stage*. New York: Summit, 1981.

Gilligan, Carol. *In a Different Voice: Psychological Theory and Women's Development*. Cambridge, MA: Harvard University Press, 1982.

Gremillion, Helen. *Feeding Anorexia: Gender and Power at a Treatment Center*. Durham, NC: Duke University Press, 2003.

Kamen, Paula. *Feminist Fatale: Voices from the "Twentysomething" Generation Explore the Future of the Women's Movement.* New York: Donald I. Fine, 1991.

Kamen, Paula. *Her Way: Young Women Remake the Sexual Revolution.* New York: New York University Press, 2000.

Myss, Carolyn. *Anatomy of the Spirit: The Seven Stages of Power and Healing.* New York: Harmony, 1996. *http://myss.com/*

Orbach, Susie. *Fat Is a Feminist Issue: The Anti-Diet Guide to Permanent Weight Loss.* New York: Berkley, 1994.

Orman, Suze. *The 9 Steps to Financial Freedom: Practical & Spiritual Steps So You Can Stop Worrying.* New York: Three Rivers Press, 2000. *http://www.suzeorman.com/*

Robbins, Alexandra, and Wilner, Abby. *Quarterlife Crisis.* New York: Tarcher/Putnam, 2001. *http://quarterlifecrisis.com*

Weingarten, Kaethe. *Common Shock: Witnessing Violence Every Day.* New York: Dutton, 2003.

Wolf, Naomi. *The Beauty Myth: How Images of Beauty Are Used Against Women.* New York: William Morrow, 1991.

WEB SITES

http://www.oprah.com
http://quarterlifecrisis.com
http://twentysomething.com

MISCELLANEOUS

Chesler, Phyllis. "Letter to a Young Feminist." Spring 1998. *http://www.phyllischesler.com/publications/letter_to_feminist.html*

Gilligan, Carol. "Joining the Resistance: Psychology, Politics, Girls and Women." *Michigan Quarterly Review* 29(1990), 501–36.

"Turbulent Twenties." *The Oprah Winfrey Show,* June 11, 2001. *http://www.oprah.com/tows/pastshows/tows_past_20010611_e.jhtml*

"What Younger Women Think About Older Women." *The Oprah Winfrey Show*, January 16, 2002. *http://www.oprah.com/tows/pastshows/tows_2002/tows_past_20020116.jhtml*

Whitehouse, Beth. "More Kids Are Coming Home to Live After College, and Their Parents, It Seems, Are Happy to Have Them." *New York Newsday*, May 23, 2002. *http://www.newsday.com/mynews/ny-p2cover2716736may23.story.*

SUGGESTIONS FROM OTHER YOUNG WOMEN

1. Find a community: an organization, church, social group, or activity club, where you can connect with people who share similar interests, ideas, and/or philosophies.

2. Create a virtual community through Web sites by joining a chat group that supports your way of thinking and shares your interests. Be mindful of selecting a group who will ally with you as you live a life that fits your values and beliefs.

3. Do volunteer work, whether in large, life-action ways, like Teach for America (*http://www.teachforamerica.org*), or in small, event-specific ways, like helping with a Thanksgiving feed-the-homeless activity.

4. Get some exercise that suits you: Go outside, walk, run, join a yoga class, play a sport.

5. Travel to different countries where you can learn about other cultures or other ways of thinking and living that may give you perspective about your own life situation.

INDEX

ABOUT THE AUTHORS

Victoria Dickerson, Ph.D., is a nationally acclaimed clinical psychologist, who, for more than twenty-five years, has specialized in working with women in their twenties and early thirties. She is an adjunct lecturer at Santa Clara University, presents workshops and lectures extensively nationally and internationally, and has taught in North America as well as Western Europe, Canada, Australia, and New Zealand. She lives in Aptos, California.

Carla Fine is the author of seven books, including *Strong, Smart, and Bold* (with Girls Inc.) and *No Time to Say Goodbye: Surviving the Suicide of a Loved One.*